WHEN EDA FRANCHI TOOK HER FIRST PILL, IT SEEMED JUST WHAT A GIRL WHO HAD EVERYTHING NEEDED—

a short-cut to the professional achievement, sexual enjoyment, and human fulfillment that should be hers.

It was a short-cut, all right—to a personal hell in which lying was a way of life, and sex was a raging, degrading need. And then the walls of madness began to close her in . . .

This is her story. She lived it. You will never forget it.

SIGNET Books You'll Want to Read

☐ **RUN, SHELLEY, RUN!** by Gertrude Samuels. More shocking and powerful than **Go Ask Alice**. A poignant, honest portrayal of a teen-age girl on the run from the sex-drug scene . . . "An important human document."—**The New York Times**
(#Y6355—$1.25)

☐ **SURVIVAL KIT by Susan B. Anthony.** While still in her teens, Susan B. Anthony started on the road to alcoholism. As a woman, she plunged into disastrous marriages and ruinous affairs. This book is the story of her survival and transcendence, and her return to work, not only for women's liberation but for human liberation.
(#Q5373—95¢)

☐ **FALLING by Susan Fromberg Schaeffer.** The heartbreaking story of a young woman's fight against a descent into madness. "I love this novel . . . the finest new talent we've seen in a long while."—**New York Times Book Review**
(#W5897—$1.50)

☐ **THE SNAKE PIT by Mary Jane Ward.** The dramatic bestseller about a young woman's mental breakdown and her torturous recovery in a state hospital for the insane. (#Y5527—$1.25)

☐ **I NEVER PROMISED YOU A ROSE GARDEN by Joanne Greenberg.** A beautifully written, bestselling novel of rare insight about a young girl's courageous fight to regain her sanity in a mental hospital. (#Y4835—$1.25)

THE NEW AMERICAN LIBRARY, INC.,
P.O. Box 999, Bergenfield, New Jersey 07621

Please send me the SIGNET BOOKS I have checked above. I am enclosing $_____(check or money order—no currency or C.O.D.'s). Please include the list price plus 25¢ a copy to cover handling and mailing costs. (Prices and numbers are subject to change without notice.)

Name_____

Address_____

City_____State_____Zip Code_____
Allow at least 3 weeks for delivery

The Long Road Back

Eda Franchi

A SIGNET BOOK
NEW AMERICAN LIBRARY
TIMES MIRROR

COPYRIGHT © 1975 BY EDA FRANCHI

All rights reserved.

 SIGNET TRADEMARK REG. U.S. PAT. OFF. AND FOREIGN COUNTRIES
REGISTERED TRADEMARK—MARCA REGISTRADA
HECHO EN CHICAGO, U.S.A.

SIGNET, SIGNET CLASSICS, MENTOR, PLUME AND MERIDIAN BOOKS
are published by The New American Library Inc.,
1301 Avenue of the Americas, New York, New York 10019.

FIRST PRINTING, MARCH, 1975

1 2 3 4 5 6 7 8 9

PRINTED IN THE UNITED STATES OF AMERICA

To Eileen

Zee

and Truett—

markers along my road.

The Long Road Back

Part One

"I'm a worthwhile person."

"Better walk around the room and say that again."

"I'm a worthwhile person. I'm a lady."

"Do you believe what you're saying?"

"No. I haven't done anything to prove it. I want to go back to law school."

"Are you ready? You've only been out of the hospital six months. It's going to be very difficult to fit into the routine of studying on your own."

"My mother has agreed to come out to Wisconsin and room with me."

"Do you want her?"

"I could use her help."

"What about Chris, your fiancé?"

"He's still in the navy. I thought it would be a good thing to have Mom to keep me company and encourage me to stay off pills."

"Are you going to stay off amphetamines? You're still taking the fifty milligrams of Thorazine that I prescribed?"

"Religiously. Only it makes me feel dopey right after I take it. As for the other question, I can't say. I can only promise to stay off pills. I still miss the little apartment I had all to myself. I decorated it and I'll never find another. I felt so bad when Mom and Chris told me that I wouldn't be able to go back and that I'd have to live in the hospital."

"You needed it, Eda. You were sick."

"I know. Even though I was straight out nuts, I still had feelings."

"What is your father going to do while you two are in Wisconsin?"

"Declare himself helpless. Aunt Gabriella will probably cook for him. It's a great sacrifice. Papa's used to Mom doing everything for him as far as housekeeping and the meals. But he's dedicated to his children."

"Do you need a doctor while you're out in Wisconsin?"

"I don't know."

"I'll see if I can recommend someone. You've progressed more rapidly than most of my patients."

That was Eda Franchi in September of 1963. I had spent one summer in the hospital with a nervous breakdown. I was a sophomore at the University of Wisconsin Law School. I had been taking amphetamines for two and a half years.

I don't know exactly why I started. But I was trying to graduate with a double major in three years, and I had been carrying eighteen to twenty-two credits a semester in an honors program. I ate a lot and was diet-conscious. I wasn't overweight, but when I faced six or seven finals a semester, I chewed on candy bars instead of my nails.

Marty, my girl friend, was taking three twenty-five-milligram tablets of Preludin a day. I expressed concern about my diet problem, and she handed me a pep pill. "Here, take one of these. You said you wanted to stay up late and study. If you're worried about weight, they'll kill your appetite and make you feel alive."

"One can't hurt."

Soon I was begging Marty for pills. Since she had a renewable prescription, I could get as many as I wanted. I took about ten pills a day and still graduated an honors student. In law school, I took many more and ended up in the hospital with a nervous breakdown.

But right now I had recovered and wanted to go back to school. Dr. Andrews warned me that if I ever went back to drugs, I might have another, more serious nervous breakdown. I didn't believe him. I was optimistic about going back to school and having Mom as a roommate. This time I would do better.

We set out for school early, in order to get settled. I never thought about what it would be like to study again without the aid of pep pills. While on the pills, I had confidence in my own ability. I kept telling myself that the side effects of an overdose, described in red on the side of the bottles, were wrong. Pills didn't affect thinking or grades. Dr. Andrews had told me that off pills, my original mental processes would return to me, and I would be the better for it. He didn't warn me that I would again feel the horrible pains of being a sensitive, ambitious, worried human being.

I signed up for five courses that semester. One of them was Civil Procedure II. When I walked into class, my sense of excitement about returning to school vanished like ice in hot oil. I was scared. Everyone looked so intelligent—so well versed in the law.

Professor Withe assembled his papers, adjusted his glasses, and called the roll. We started with the thirty-page assignment that had been given ahead of time. Subject: *Res judicata, plea in bar,* and *estoppel.* His words passed over my head.

"From the blank looks on your faces I can tell that everyone has read this assignment. How many of you have read the assignment? Raise your hands."

I had read the assignment, but I didn't raise my hand. I was afraid that he would ask me a question. One hand went up.

"I thought so. I see that I'll have to spoon-feed you until Wednesday when you've all *read the assignment.*"

I furiously copied down every word that Professor Withe said. I didn't understand, but I wrote down the words anyway. That had been my practice while on pills: copy down everything that the man had to say; recopy it because it was barely readable; tie it up with the text and eventually understand the main principles involved.

I went to the four other courses and picked up a total of 130 pages of reading between Monday and Wednesday. When I got back, Mom was waiting with a cup of hot chocolate.

"How did you do, dear?"

"Ma, I can't."

"You've been saying that all along, dear, but you have."

"I'm going to flunk Civil Procedure—flamboyantly flunk."

"Eda, it's only your first day. You've always said that you'd flunk. I remember when you used to call us long distance."

"I know. Papa says that I never failed him."

"And you never did. You always got A's."

"That was undergrad. This is law school. An idiot can graduate from undergrad."

"And be an honors student? And do it in three years? And take the lead role in four plays that are in foreign languages? And win the Portuguese poetry contest for original composition when you'd only had one year of the language and were competing against doctoral candidates? Eda, think of all the things that you did."

"I was happier my last year."

"Eda, you didn't do anything while you were on drugs. Your grades fell, and you dropped out of all the extra-curricular activities. You resigned as vice-president of the Spanish honors society. You turned down roles in the Italian plays."

"I became dedicated to law."

"You became tied up in busywork. Papa and I thought that something was wrong, but we didn't know what. No, Eda, don't ever say that you want to go back on drugs."

"Ma, I'm scared. I've been out a semester, and I'm slow."

"Is it the medication that you're taking?"

"I don't know. Honest, Ma, I didn't understand a thing that Withe said today. I don't want to go on Wednesday. I've read the assignment fifty pages ahead, but I don't understand *res judicata,* or *equitable estoppel.* I only understand *plea in bar.*"

"Then you understand one thing, and that's a starting point."

Chris called that night. "Eda, how is school?"

"Awful. I'm going to flunk. I wish that you were here to bellywack down Bascom in the snow."

The tears started streaming from my eyes.

"Eda, do your best. Do your best for me."

I hung up the phone and leaned my head against the wall, sobbing.

Mom looked at me. "Eda, you shouldn't make Chris feel so bad."

The lump in my throat grew bigger. "I miss him so. We spent so many winters on that hill. Every time it thaws, I think that any minute he's going to splash me with that damn fenderless bike. I'm left with all the ghosts of last year. I saw Jesse Stewart today. Jesse only knew me when I was on pep pills. We used to study together. He says he can't believe the change that's taken place."

"Eda, don't worry about what everyone else thinks."

I studied extra hard for Civil Pro that week. I volunteered answers. Professor Withe saw that I was trying. I would stay after class to listen to him explain the fine points, but I was basically convinced that I didn't understand.

Three weeks after the semester began, Dean Fox called me into his office. "Sit down, Eda. Tell me why you came back to law school."

"I want to be a lawyer."

"It's not the greatest thing in the world. I worked in New York City and finally decided that I didn't want it."

"But I want that degree."

"There are lots of law-trained people who aren't lawyers."

"Let me try again."

"Professor Ogden came to me last semester with some of the letters that you had written—Why do flowers die? Because people say they will.—Do you believe that any more?"

"No. I'm all right. I was on drugs for the past two years. If I stay off them, I'll be able to do better."

Dean Fox kept pressing me.

"But, Eda, law is frustrating if you're not dedicated."

"I'm a good student. I'll prove it to you."

We shook hands, and I left the office. I dismissed the interview and went home to Mom.

"Ma, I'll take a short nap before dinner."

"Tired?"

"No. But maybe if I fall asleep, I'll get away from all this for a little while. Then I'll be fresher for studying."

I went into the bedroom, flopped down on my stomach, but didn't go to sleep. As I toyed with the long fringe on the bedspread, I thought about all the letters that I had written to my professors before I left for home. I had read some of them when I got out of the hospital—letters that I hadn't mailed—and I was scared. At the time, I had thought they were the words of God given unto me, His prophet. Now they made no sense.

I rolled the long pieces of fringe through my fingers and started folding them into flat braids. Two years of twisted anxiety had passed. I wanted to unravel those letters and start again. I caught the fringe on a hangnail, undid the braids, and answered Mom's call to dinner.

The baked chicken smelled delicious, but I was afraid to touch it. Without my pills, I was afraid to touch anything. I wanted to lose weight.

"Eda, you're not fat. You have a nice slim figure."

"I don't want to get fat."

"You could have a teaspoon of potatoes."

"No! No potatoes."

"All those vegetables just bloat you. Papa says it's not good to eat so much roughage. As a doctor, he knows."

"I can't eat too much tonight anyway because I have to study Civil Pro."

After dinner, I helped Mom with the dishes. I didn't want to open the Civil Pro book. Mom was worried.

"Eda, you are different. Before you started with pills, you used to tackle the most difficult things. Impossibility was all the more incentive for you to try."

"Civil Pro is over my head, Mom."

"Maybe you ought to see a doctor. I've been with you for three weeks and school is getting you down."

"See who you can find. I'll still take the Thorazine, but I think I'm getting a bad reaction."

Mom found Dr. Marlow. He was the director of the state mental institution and the best in his field.

My appointment with Dr. Marlow, scheduled for the next week, couldn't come soon enough. Perhaps he could prescribe something to lift me out of my misery. By the time I got into his office, I was close to tears. By the time I finished, I was the mask of tragedy, accented by two black lines of mascara running down my cheeks.

Dr. Marlow didn't say anything until the end of the interview. I didn't give him a chance.

"I'm flunking, Dr. Marlow—flunking. I was on amphetamines for the past two years and had a nervous breakdown. I want to finish law school. But it's so much more difficult now that I'm off pep pills. Dr. Andrews in Syracuse told me that my head would be clearer—that now I could reason and think. Instead, I worry and cry. I miss my fiancé Chris. Yet I wanted to go back to school. It's just that I started feeling everything. I walk around campus like a sick basset hound. Mom cooks up the most delicious meals, but my fork turns to lead under the fear of gaining weight. Without my pills, I can't eat."

After I'd finished my long monologue, Dr. Marlow put down his pen.

"Why the concern with grades? Why such drive for perfection?"

"Because I was that way once. I've always gotten honors. But now—now I read . . . I think I understand . . . I go to class the next day and find out that I missed all the fine points."

"Part of your difficulty, Eda, is lack of confidence in your ability."

"But on pep pills I understood everything that was said. I was happy."

"No. Those pills give you a feeling of self-confidence. It's fake. Now you're back to what caused you to go on them in the first place."

"What was that?"

"Eda, I don't know you very well. Offhand you strike me as a person who has had extraordinary scholastic success. Nevertheless, you have an overwhelming fear of failure. And, from the way your mother described your language ability and all your other interests, it seems that pep pills narrowed you down to one field. I'd like to talk at the next meeting about your goals and your family."

"Can you help me?"

"I can't help you pass courses. But I'm going to change your medication. I'll have to experiment with what you take from now on. Try this for a week and let me know how you feel."

I took the new medication that night and went to bed. If I slept, the effect was purely psychological. At nine o'clock the next day, I sat in Civil Pro. I started taking notes, but my fingers began to twitch uncontrollably. My jaw locked tight and my lips pursed. The adrenaline was pumping double-time through my veins. I wasn't listening to Professor Withe. His voice became an echo in a tunnel of bells that chimed in discord through my brain. It must have been those new pills. I had to call Dr. Marlow right away.

"Dr. Marlow, I'm ready to jump out of my skin. These pills make me so worried and restless that I can't see straight. I'm inhuman."

"It may take a while, Eda. Try them for the next few days. If you don't get any better results, call me. I can't understand it. I prescribed a milder tranquilizer and antidepressant."

"If this doesn't work, Doctor, I have a suggestion. Tofranil. Have you ever heard of it? Papa used to give it to me at home when I got upset. Of course, he didn't know that I was on amphetamines."

"Eda, try the first medication and see if you can't hang on until your appointment next week."

I took my dosage of the new pills for three days and then capitulated. Mom was exhausted from the unrelenting vigil of tears, midnight walks, and the final glass of sherry to tone me down. I called Dr. Marlow again.

"Dr. Marlow, the pills that you gave me make me feel like I'm on amphetamines again. I'm so nervous, and I can't think straight. I haven't opened a book in three days."

"You mentioned before that you had been on Tofranil. Do you think it might help?"

"I'm willing to try."

"Then come and talk to me this evening. I've rearranged my schedule."

Dr. Marlow was very kind, and again I was on my way to thinking that my anxiety would be cured by the use of the pills. He wanted to talk about Papa.

"What was he like, Eda?"

"Papa was first in his class at Buffalo Med school. He came to this country without a penny and is now worth about seven million dollars. He plays the stock market. The brokers are always calling him for advice on what to buy. He's a surgeon and chief of staff at one of the hospitals in our city."

"But what does he think of you?"

"He's proud of me. I'm the only one in the family who's going to be a professional. My sister Stella applied to law school but got married instead. Papa didn't want her to. He was afraid that men were after the Franchi girls for their money. Besides, her husband wasn't a professional. My sister Angelina eloped with Roy in her sophomore year at Syracuse University. Papa threatened to go down to Texas and sue Roy under the Mann Act. It was a lot of grief. Papa always picked on my brother Luciano because he never studied and showed no signs of even getting to college. Rocco, my youngest brother, might go to medical school if his grades are high enough. I'm the only one left. The only time that I failed Papa was when I went on drugs and ended up in the hospital."

"Did your father ever ask you why you went on amphetamines?"

"No. I thought he was going to bawl the hell out of me. Papa was used to bawling us out. Sometimes he'd come home looking for a fight. He'd end up ranting at the top of his lungs that we were all a bunch of goddamn-no-good-spoiled-brat-bastards and that he was going to leave us all and sell the house. Mom would usually end up in tears."

"Did he bawl you out for taking drugs?"

"No. When he came to the hospital, I saw a side of Papa that I had never known. He was kind and wanted to help me. He's like that in the office and that's why his patients call him *combodi*, relative by blood."

"You're either angry at your father or afraid of him."

"I guess I'm the only one who took his orders seriously."

"Why did you go to law school?"

"I graduated from college in three years. I had a choice —I won a scholarship to go to Brazil or I could go to law school. I wanted another general field of study, and law sounded like a real challenge. And now I'm flunking. I feel it in my bones, and it follows me like a double shadow."

"Have you ever flunked a course?"

"Once."

"Are you on pep pills now?"

"No. Can't you tell? I haven't smiled or laughed since I quit a year ago. I'm on Tofranil."

"Do they help you?"

"Somewhat. Mom says it's all a matter of positive thinking."

"It's time to stop now. Continue your dosage of Tofranil. You've built an image of your father as king. Are you trying to prove yourself to him? You set your own standards so high that no human could live up to them. Tell me, do you think that you're a worthwhile person? Could you be a worthwhile person without being a lawyer?"

"No and no. Don't ask me why. My mind is missile-set —it knows no other direction."

Mom and I flew home during semester break. Papa was overjoyed. Of course we had to go to his office and see his sister, Aunt Gabriella. She lived in an apartment that was part of Papa's office.

Aunt Gabriella had prepared a Sicilian feast: pasta with clam sauce, followed by roast lamb with a side dish of buttered artichokes, mushrooms, and fresh baby peas, crusty homemade bread and wine, all topped off with rum-glazed cheesecake—the works. She was a marvelous cook, and the table groaned under the weight of so many delicacies. Gabriella always made too much and ate too much: she was five feet four and weighed close to two hundred pounds. Along with Papa, she was a perpetual calorie counter. When Gabriella brought the food, Papa would count the calories out loud or protest that she had given him too much. Nevertheless, his plate was clean at the end. Papa never praised a good meal without concluding that he would skip lunch the next day. We'd often have to stop at the office before going out so that Papa could get on the scales and tell the whole family how much he had gained or lost. No one paid any attention to this fetish except me. It seeped slowly into my receptive mind, and, over the years, solidified into a massive phobia that soured every bite with the fear of gaining an ounce.

I visited with Aunt Gabriella a few minutes and then said I wanted to get weighed. It was a Saturday, and the office was empty. I walked through the long corridor into the examining room, and on the table beside all the medicines was Papa's prescription pad. It was so easy. It had always been easy. Now, with that big meal awaiting me, it was automatic. I walked over to the table, listened for sounds, and quickly grabbed the prescription pad. My hands were sweating and my heart was beating fast. My conscience was telling me: Eda, no! He forgave me once —but again? I didn't listen. Why not be happy? I'm miserable now. I can't look at anything without counting the goddamn calories. No one will know—not even Dr. Marlow. I have to regain my sanity.

I opened up my blouse and stuffed half a pad of prescriptions in my bra. Then I got weighed. I had gained two pounds since school began. I returned to Gabriella's apartment, went to the bathroom, and transferred the prescription pad from my bra to the zippered pocket in my purse. Relieved, I went out and picked at the meal. Papa praised Gabriella's cooking and asked for seconds.

"Gabriella, this is delicious; you're an excellent cook. What's the matter, Eda, aren't you hungry?"

"I've had enough."

"You filled up on all those vegetables. Why don't you have some more meat? You didn't even touch your spaghetti."

"Spaghetti's fattening."

"Eda, you're not fat."

"I'm not fat. But I'm full."

"You could gain another ten pounds. You'd look better if you had a little fat on you. You have no hips, girl."

"Papa, I'm okay. Full—stuffed—*basta.*"

That was enough. The next day, I told Mom that I wanted to look at some new dresses and went downtown. I walked absentmindedly between the chattering bargain hunters telling myself that I'd been through a lot. Then I went into the department store bathroom, sat on the john, and pulled the preseription pad out of my purse. I wrote in Papa's worst but still legible handwriting: "150 Preludin 25 mg. T.I.D. Refills x 3", signed it, folded it carefully, and went into a big discount drug house. I was given a number and I told the pharmacist that I would be back in twenty minutes.

I returned to the department store, oblivious of the people crowding in after lunch for late afternoon sales. Would the pharmacist call Papa to clarify the handwriting —to confirm the prescription? I picked up a pair of gloves at the sale counter, tried them on, and told myself no. I had done it many times before. The drugstore never checked unless the prescription was over the phone. They never cross-checked, so I could go to another pharmacy the next week and start another prescription. I put down the gloves, checked the time, and went back for my magic package.

Later, in the john, I emptied the pills into the lining of my purse. I kept the label with the store name and date of prescription so that I wouldn't go back for a refill too soon. I calculated roughly, wrote the prospective date of return on the label, and tucked it away.

I took a pill and continued my calculations. I had approximately twenty prescriptions with three refills on each one. That would get me through the end of the semester. I could count on Tofranil or anything else in the family house to get me to sleep. Papa kept barbiturate samples in the bathroom drawers, phenobarbital in his top drawer, and a huge jar of Deprol on his dresser. I took another pep pill just to be sure that I would be feeling better. I also wanted to dull the effects of the Tofranil.

As I walked out of the department store, I could feel my old energy returning. My throat was dry, so I stopped for a cup of coffee. I looked at the tired, blank faces around me. I saw a middle-aged matron in the corner scrape up the remaining chocolate from a hot fudge sundae and told myself that I was right. I was Eda, made of gossamer wings, light as silk. I could wake up again without the loaded feeling of being on tranquilizers. I'd be interested, active, and bright. The matron finished her dessert, wobbled off the chair, and picked up her shopping bags. I looked at her apron of fat and vowed to stay on amphetamines until I lost twenty pounds. I'd only take three Preludin a day and would eventually quit.

Mom picked me up that afternoon.

"Did you find anything, dear?"

"No. Most of the styles didn't appeal to me. But, sweetie, why don't you come with me tomorrow, and we'll go down to that designer shop together?"

"Gee, Eda. You're enthusiastic."

"What the hell, Mom. We have to go back to school in a few days."

Since the people that I had known—including my fiancé—were more used to me on pills than off, it was impossible for them to tell that I had started again. I had to be careful this time. I had to keep my temper in line. I had to eat enough to keep everyone happy.

Mom and I went shopping the next day. In the meantime, I kept down to three pills a day. I gradually began to lose weight. Papa noticed, but Mom must have talked him into keeping his mouth shut.

During the remaining time at home, I made up my mind to study. I didn't understand Civil Pro, but now I could devote much more time to it. I read at night after most of the family had gone to bed, and to get to sleep quickly I took a Deprol or phenobarbital. The next day I would wake up and immediately pop a pill on my way downstairs for six cups of breakfast coffee. By then I was feeling like my old self.

Mom and I departed for Wisconsin two days later, and I packed the prescriptions in the lining of my purse. I had been to another drugstore and now had around two hundred pills to last me until the end of the semester. I vowed not to tell Dr. Marlow or anyone that I was back on drugs.

My next visit to Dr. Marlow was different. He thought that the rest at home had given me a needed change and more confidence in myself.

"Eda, you seem more enthusiastic."

"I am, but have no hope of passing Civil Pro this semester."

"I'd still like to figure out why you're so concerned over getting good grades. Is it because you've always gotten good grades in the past?"

"I don't know. Papa spent the vacation trying to be friendly to me. But he hurt my feelings."

"Want to tell me about it?"

"Papa's always saying that we don't appreciate him. But I think he pays no attention to us. We were discussing estate planning. Papa said that his will is old and asked me about what to do. Since I couldn't handle it, I told him what to think about. I explained all the intricacies of estate taxation and planning. It was my best course. I got the second highest grade in the class and was up on the subject. I spent two hours with him on it and what does he say in the end. 'Well, Eda, that's more than I wanted to know. I'll consult Ralph about it. He'll know what to do better than you and me.' At that point, Dr. Marlow, I said nothing. Ralph is an editor of law books who practices part-time at the firm where I worked last summer. Why the hell didn't Papa ask Ralph in the first place if he had all the answers? Why pick my brains and then go running to Ralph who was so sure to charge him a fee for my efforts? Brag—brag—brag about me. But when it comes down to actually taking advantage of what I've learned, Papa turns to those who have made a name for themselves. In Papa's book, I have no status."

"Did you know that you have a lot of hostility toward your father?"

"We're two of a kind. My nickname at home used to be Mulehead. I'm just as temperamental and ambitious as he is. But he's the last one to see all these traits in his own kid."

"How old are you now?"

"Twenty-three. Our relationship has always been stormy. Mom has to negotiate with Papa on behalf of us, her kids. She convinces him to decide in our favor without subjecting him to the indignity of spoiling his children. Papa has everything from breakfast in bed to hand-pressed shirts on two minutes' notice. Mom never complains about his absolute dependency in household matters."

"What about your fiancé?"

"He's different. He feels it's unfair to expect me to handle all the housework. He knows it's unwise to call it woman's work because I hate it. I want to be a lawyer. That's why I went through college in three years, and I intend to get my law degree before I get married. Hell, I didn't even want to get engaged."

"You've never had intercourse?"

"No, and I don't intend to until I get married and I have to. It doesn't sound very interesting."

"How long have you been dating Chris?"

"About five years."

"Do you masturbate?"

"I guess not," I lied. "I don't know much about sex. Nobody ever told me."

"Never mind, Eda, that's enough for now. You have your own definite ideas. They aren't wrong. Sexually, you seem to have no problems."

Dr. Marlow was wrong. Since I had resumed the pills, I was turned on all the time. My vagina itched constantly. In the past, Chris and I had petted. He couldn't understand my ability to reach a climax two or three times in the course of an evening when all he did was kiss and fondle my breasts. Now that I was alone, the scene was different. I had an animal craving to be satisfied.

I was worried about Mom on the nights that I masturbated. I didn't want her to hear the moving about in the bed, the right finger in the right spot, and the animal panting when I achieved satisfaction.

Later on, my sexual drives got stronger. I would be

studying in the ladies' lounge at the law school. I'd get hot, go into the john and hope that no one else came. I'd quickly pull down my pants, cuss myself for being such a little bitch, a few twists in the right spot and I was relieved.

Exam time was coming, and I cut down on the pills enough to concentrate and pass my subjects. I cried a little before I went into the Civil Pro final and made it through the other exams with lots of tears. I had my last meeting with Dr. Marlow and was told that there was no need for continued therapy. I had recovered. This was confirmed when I received my grades. I had passed all my courses—including Civil Pro! In one more year I'd be a lawyer. I was happy, but I had breached a trust.

The summer passed quickly, but signs of taking the pills began to show. My facial hair grew out in thick, blunt stubs. I developed a moustache and sideburns, which I eliminated with a depilatory. No one noticed.

But the other symptoms of taking amphetamines didn't go away so easily. My teeth ached daily and began to decay underneath the caps. I had had two sets of crowns and badly needed another set. My gums receded, leaving pockets of undigested food and inflamed tissues. Mom and I went to a specialist for X-rays. I had developed pyorrhea. We had to make plans, and the only question was timing. I would return to Syracuse for a three-month ordeal after the wedding. I had to have root canal work on every tooth in my upper jaw and a complete restoration of every tooth in my mouth. Half of it was due to bad dentists, but the other half was due to amphetamines. I rarely brushed my teeth. Mom had to remind me when my breath was bad or when my clothes smelled of sweat. I considered these secondary to my studies.

Other signs of being addicted went unnoticed. I was supposed to be at the law firm at nine o'clock every morning. Instead, I waited for a ride with someone in the family and wouldn't show until eleven or noon. As I increased my dosage, my work pattern became more haphazard. I was supposed to write briefs or draft complaints. I did minor detective work. The firm knew that I was a convincing liar, so I got the job of searching out people for collection. Most of the time, however, I did nothing. I would arrange all my working materials, pop a few pills, and read the editorials in *The New York Times*. When I worked, I found that the effects of the pills were even interfering with my approach to the basic issues of law practice. I became too involved in learning all the principles of law at once and trying to pour them into one case.

One day Ralph asked me to draw up a complaint about an auto accident. He gave me a complaint from a similar case to follow, so the assignment was simple. I spent an hour sharpening pencils, refilling the stapler, drawing extra margins on the legal pad, and removing dirt from my fingernails by peeling them down to the quick. Then I copied the first paragraph from my model and inserted the names of the people involved. I read the standard paragraph alleging that someone got hurt: "The Plaintiff was bruised, injured, and suffered shock and contusions. She suffered pain on and about her body, nausea—all to her damage in the sum of $10,000." The whole thing was wordy, unrealistic, and superficial. I drafted the paragraph in my own words and went in to see Ralph.

"Ralph, I thought you wanted a more detailed description of the injuries."

"Eda, if I don't use the standard phrases, they'll hold me to the specific allegations just as you have drafted them. It will limit what I can introduce as proof."

"But it doesn't make any sense to say that the plaintiff was badly bruised in and about her body and all that garbage."

"Eda, don't work so hard. We're lucky if we get a $500 settlement in this case."

"Ralph, these complaints aren't even written in the King's English. They're redundant and grammatically bad. They stink."

"Eda, dear. Sit down. Let me tell you something. It doesn't make any difference. That's the way the courts of

New York want those complaints and that's the way we've been doing them for years. I know you're a purist. When I got out of law school ten years ago I was the same way. My first boss had to tell me the same thing. Law practice is different from law school. It's a make-money business."

"Okay, I'll copy the last complaint. But it hurts to have been an honors English student and turn out such bastardized stuff."

I did the complaint over again, but inside I was sick. A secretary could have done the work. I was out to make new law or find something out of the ordinary. As with my home life, everything had to be novel and unusual. It had to be an "Eda," a creation all my own.

In the meantime, I wasn't convinced that the law firm wanted me. Papa had been referring all his accident cases to the firm since I started work, so I was never sure of accomplishing anything in my own name. Instead, it was the natural outcome of being Dr. Franchi's daughter. I was always introduced as the daughter of Dr. Franchi, following in his professional footsteps to become a lawyer.

I took two weeks off before the beginning of the next semester. I'd stop by to visit Aunt Gabriella at the office on Thursdays—Papa's day off—and build my supply of prescriptions for the next semester. Everyone in the family was pleased that I took the time to visit Aunt Gabriella.

I packed my clothes for school and then I packed my pills. Inside the lining of my purse were enough blank prescriptions to last until the semester break. I had also accumulated about one hundred pills, just in case there was a delay at the local drugstore. I was taking fourteen pills a day and was anxious to get back to school.

I moved into a coed graduate dorm with apartment suites housing four to a unit. The place was modern, sterile, compact, and overpriced. I was the first one to arrive; I spent hours hanging clothes in order of color, placing books in order of size, and hiding pills in different locations for easy access. When Vivian, my roommate, arrived, I chatted for a few minutes and then we went over to the law school. I saw Jesse Stuart, gave him my new address, and told him I would call to see what classes we had in common. He said I seemed more like my old self and that he would be ready to start reviewing after the first week.

I had always studied well with Jesse. He was intelligent, extremely handsome, and a confirmed bachelor. I was his envied confidante on dating issues, too. Jesse had been to bed with so many girls that he was spoiled. I warned him that when he met a girl with brains enough to ignore him, he'd fall like a California redwood before her pink, powdered feet. He laughed, gave me a squeeze, and went down to buy books.

I returned to the dorm. Three boys roomed across the hall, and one—Rex Slater—was a freshman law student. His roommates, Nat and Mike, were chem grad students. It was flattering to have men around. I always preferred them to women. They were more devoted—more career-minded.

As I took more pills, my career ambitions grew. I avoided discussions with friends who wanted to dedicate their lives to helping their man get ahead. Mom had been that way. She had stayed at home, raised five children, and mastered the domestic arts. But Mom was different from the hungry, cooing, helpless spinsters at school.

By the time that classes began, I had already read three chapters ahead in each course; I started to look around for unassigned material. I looked up *Law Review* articles and took very detailed notes in class, which I rewrote to put them in more presentable form and to memorize them for review. In short, I overstudied. I didn't learn anything; I was memorizing. My reasoning power had diminished slowly under the influence of the pills and my study time had increased. I was taking fifteen pills a day, and all that concerned me were grades and finals.

My roommates were amazed at my inexhaustible energy. At midnight I was wide awake. Nat was still up, and we soon made a habit of nightly walks around campus that lasted until one or two in the morning. Nat and I would walk at a fast clip aroud the engineering campus or to the barns in the agricultural school to see if any of the cows were still out. He wanted to get a doctorate in organic chemistry and become a professor. He liked to hear about the trivia that I had picked up in *The Times* and he laughed at my opinionated outlook on women. Nat was also interested in my roommate, Vivian, and I encouraged him to ask her out. He was a perfect match and, as with Jesse, I knew when I was right.

I also talked with Rex Slater who walked me to classes at law school. I loaned him my notes from my freshman courses. They were elaborate recopies, not-a-word-missed notes. Rex just went to class, sat down, and flipped the pages. The content of the courses had changed very little.

Sometimes, after eleven hours of grind at the books, I would suggest to Rex that we go to the pub for a pitcher of beer and a chaser. He was usually short of funds so I picked up the tab. It was worth it. I considered Rex one of my close friends and a safe escort. The pub was always noisy and crowded. We'd find a place, he'd get the beer, and as two business partners, we'd talk law while the jukebox played "I Can't Wait Forever." I loved that song and wasted quarter after quarter on the music, which made me free, light, able to glide over mundane preoccupations.

The beer usually made me tipsy, and Rex was always gentleman enough to grab hold of my arm and escort me to the dorm around the corner. Vivian understood, but roommate Harriet thought the whole matter scandalous. She told me that an engaged girl had no business going out with a single man. She failed to grasp my intent. I never thought of my relationships with Rex, Nat, or Jesse in a sexual light. We flirted, but there was something deeper; we respected each other. I cherished my independence. Harriet was only feeling left-out and jealous, I decided.

Jesse and I started our review sessions for Bankruptcy. He came to the dorm every Sunday night, and we'd grind at the principles of law for three or four hours. He also had ulterior motives for coming to the dorm. Edith Donne, his latest, lived downstairs. She had told Jesse to wait while she made up her mind about a fellow she was currently dating. Jesse had been refused. He was curious and jealous.

"Eda, I don't want you to meet her. You're two of a kind—independent and smart. You might give her ideas."

"She doesn't need any, Jesse, she's doing exactly what I told you to watch out for."

"Have you seen her with anyone—I mean—a man?"

"How can I tell? I don't even know what she looks like."

"Slim, long brown hair, sparkling eyes, fickle! Damn her! Let's get back to the notes."

I kept my routine of going to different drugstores, refilling prescriptions. I usually knew the druggist, but never waited while the prescription was being filled. Instead, I'd find a bookstore and load up on multicolored pencils to use in underlining my overdecorated notes. I didn't want my classmates or my roommate Vivian to know. I'd return to the drugstore around twenty minutes later and pick up my magic pills. As the pressure rose during finals, I upped my dosage to twenty pills a day.

My appetite increased as did those moments of complete exhaustion. On Sundays I slept till five in the afternoon and dragged through classes the next day. I was slipping, but it was almost the end of the semester. Then, one night, I had a "frozen dream."

I lay in bed quiet, feeling the pins of numbness slowly penetrate and paralyze my limbs. My eyes were closed, and yet before me stood Boots Ryan, the black rapist, who had scaled the fire escape at a girls' dorm three years ago and threatened a coed with the same razor blade that he now held in one gloved hand. I called out for help, but the words echoed against the bedroom door. My former roommate, whom I hadn't seen in two years, entered the room. I begged her for help, but she only stared with pitiful, sympathetic eyes. Boots moved closer and laid the razor against my throat. I writhed back and forth, but the nerves in my back were paralyzed, sending painful chills up my spine. I was conscious and unconscious—living and dying at the same time. I mustered up all the strength remaining in my body and moved my head back and forth to shake out of it. I had to stop the dull pounding in my head and wake up. Boots faded into the background with a hysterical laugh. I was still numb, but awake, exhausted and afraid to go back to sleep. The dream was one of many that I had had in previous times. The visions that passed before my eyes in the paralyzed state were always horrifying. Later, when I was in the hospital, they sent me, shaking and in tears, to the nearest nurse.

I had some Deprol with me and took it that night to get to sleep. I awoke in a groggy state the next day and popped four pep pills before going to final review classes. The "frozen dream" was only a nonrecurring side effect of taking 500 milligrams of Preludin.

Finals arrived, and the steady review with Jesse paid off. I beat Jesse by one point, getting 91 in Bankruptcy. I told myself that, "frozen dreams" or not, I was in good shape.

By this time, I had found a valuable combination. It kept me on amphetamines a long time. I'd go to bed after my nightly walks with Nat with two sleeping pills and wake up with two or three pep pills in the morning. When I ran out of sleeping pills, I'd go down to the pub with Rex for a pitcher of beer, music, and a tipsy trip home.

My roommates knew nothing of the sleeping pills; understood the walks with Nat; and winced at my trips to the pub with Rex. Vivian admired my drive. Her attitude encouraged me, and, combined with my high grades for the semester, sent me packing home in a good mood.

Two days at home and I was restless for the freedom that I had enjoyed at school. Papa talked about the stock market, which bored me, or broke the silence by asking me if I was taking anything. Mom noted that I was antagonistic and made a point of disagreeing with him on many issues. So I kept my mouth shut, since the conversations with Papa were more a formality than a pleasure.

On this visit home I also made a trip to the dermatologist. My skin wasn't particularly bad, but blemishes were forming—big pussy ones. The doctor recommended a lotion and a dosage of antibiotics, which I bought but never took. The lotion, combined with the amphetamines, caused havoc. When my skin broke out even more and began to peel, I discontinued the use of that as well as regular skin care. Yet, I still had confidence in my looks. Men on the street turned as I walked by, noting the slender figure in fashionable clothes.

Mom, determined that I shouldn't be so bookish, talked me into a trip to the hairdresser's. Donna, the manicurist, was appalled at my nails. I peeled them down to the quick whenever I was nervous. Donna was a great reader and movie-goer. We talked all the time that I was under the dryer about what to see or read.

Later, when Donna had the chance, she summed up my behavior in a comment to Mom. It all came back to me at home: "Eda, you're talking a lot lately. You talk very fast. Donna even said that your rapid rambling left her completely enervated."

"Mom, I'm embarrassed by silence. I want to fill it in."

"But, dear, you exhaust yourself and everybody else."

"People are there for conversation. When I don't want them, I go and rest."

"Eda, you're always so hurried. We have trouble following your train of thought. You skip from one thing to another. I guess you're just too enthusiastic."

I left my parents and returned to school early for my last semester. In June I would graduate, and in August I would marry Chris Spaight. Chris was in the navy, and I hadn't seen him for months. I didn't miss him either. On pills, I lacked those emotions which tear into the soul and make one human. I had written Chris whenever I had the chance, and I received love letters from him daily. When I arrived back at school, a letter was waiting. I opened it carefully and read:

Eda, I know you're confused and upset about our goals. Everyone is telling you what to do, and you're wondering whether you're doing the right thing. When we get married, honey, you can do what you want, and I'll be behind you. Whatever you do is right. I've never met a girl with so much ambition and talent. I love you, Eda, so much that you'll never know. I miss your laughter and bright personality. When we get married, I want you with me always....

I folded the letter, placed it on the stack of unanswered mail labeled "incoming," and vowed that my last semester would be my best semester. I started to prepare early and signed up for nine credits. In three months I would be a lawyer. My roommate Vivian had also had a successful grade average. Rex Slater almost flunked out of law school. He blamed this on our nightly visits to the pub. I was disappointed and afraid they might soon end. Even today, when I hear hip, turned-on rock with a good beat, I think of the times in the pub when, for a few moments, I was free, and all within me goes wild. Rex was going to study harder, so we agreed to limit the trips to the pub to one night a week.

As the semester progressed, my dosage increased to twenty-five pills or 615 milligrams of Preludin a day. It was showing. My letters to my parents and to Chris became more infrequent. I was more restless, and my appetite increased to the point of six doughnuts for breakfast, two sandwiches for lunch, and double helpings at dinner.

Yet, despite all my eating, I never gained weight. I was awake day and night and slept, on the average, about four hours. When I didn't sleep, I was recopying my notes. I spent less time studying and more time organizing. Easter vacation was coming, and I was in dire need of a break.

In the meantime, I called home to discuss the final arrangements for the wedding and graduation plans. I flew to New York City during the vacation and picked out a gown. Mom mailed out all of the invitations, and I crossed the wedding off my mind until finals were over. Grades were again on my mind, and getting the law degree was of primary importance.

Vivian arrived back from vacation first. She had spent two days at Nat's place. They were much closer now, and I knew that soon I would have no nightly walks with Nat. I bowed out gracefully, since all was going as I said it would. But when Vivian and Nat had a misunderstanding, I was always called on as intermediary.

A few weeks before finals, I increased my dosage of pep pills to twenty-seven pills or 675 milligrams of Preludin a day. I was getting high. My excuse: I couldn't stop. I knew the consequences of stopping and was too close to obtaining my degree. Besides, it was too late and too embarrassing to tell anyone—including my future husband Chris. He might take my pills away.

My basic drives began to weaken. I was uptight most of the time and slept only after a heavy dosage of nonprescription sleeping pills—I had already exhausted the supply of barbiturates that I had brought from home.

Physically, I was becoming a wreck. My teeth ached constantly, and I neglected to brush them. My skin broke out and large welts were forming under my chin—large, ugly, pussy, itchy welts. Since I was nervous, I scratched them unconsciously, which made matters worse. My facial hair grew longer. I had to pluck my moustache twice a week as well as the inch-long hairs on the side of my face. My mouth was always pursed, my lips puckered in a smirk and my jaw tight. I talked a mile a minute and was constantly restless and bored.

My mental state was a different story. I lived law so much that I became law-engrossed. Talk about other things bored me. I was impatient and worried about things going smoothly from the moment I got up until the first dosage of pills. After they took effect, I was happy. If I went off amphetamines now, the only way was down.

I didn't want to go down, so I increased my dosage to thirty pills or 750 milligrams of Preludin a day. I was so high that nothing concerned me. If Harriet started arguing, I usually walked away. If anyone said anything that I strongly disagreed with, I left the scene.

I soon reached the point where I stopped counting the number of pills I took. When the bottle was half empty, I went down to the drugstore for a refill. I now had a long list of all the drugstores and the time when it was safe to return. To minimize suspicion, I had to go across town for supplies. I began splitting the pills in halves and quarters. I would take a bite whenever I needed extra pep. In addition, I was thirsty for coffee. I drank fifteen to twenty cups a day.

By this time, I began to feel powerful. I was exhilarated most of the time and cheerful to everyone. I liked to make people laugh, and it became a game to say or do unusual things. Eda Franchi had to stand out and be different from everyone else.

When finals arrived, I had volumes to cram into my head. It was more difficult now to see the basic theories that I had studied. I resolved not to increase my dosage and devoted the remainder of the time to outlining and memorizing my notes.

Exam week was hectic. Competition was stiff and everyone was looking around, worried about what everyone else was doing. I got lost and hung out in the geography library of my undergrad days. It was reassuring to study tucked away at a desk between the stacks of books with nothing to break the silence but the ticking of a fifty-year-old wall clock. I arrived at each exam two minutes before starting time and usually stayed until I got a quiet tap on the shoulder telling me that my time was up.

I walked out of Insurance, my last final, like a wounded doe, convinced that I had flunked. Instead of brooding over such a grim result, I took Rex by the arm and went down to the pub. The ordeal was over.

I decided to relax and went off pills. I slept two days straight—heavy, exhausting, sweaty sleep. Then I went down to the drugstore for a refill. I was too accustomed to being awake. When I slept, I was missing something.

Three days later, I received the news that I had passed. I would soon graduate. Mom and Papa arrived the next day to celebrate. Chris was coming the following day.

I was now a lawyer. I had done what everyone in the family had doubted. From the day of my arrival at the university, my relatives had predicted that I would find a man, get married, and stay home to raise children. Chris bet me fifty dollars that I would be married before I was twenty-four. Inwardly, I fought all these predictions. What right did people have to judge me by the standards they set for themselves? Why did they persist in their smug assumptions that I would eventually conform?

I kept my thoughts to myself and confided in Chris. I never asked people to accept my ways and only wanted them to tolerate me. Most of the boys in law school thought that woman's place was in the home. I never cared what they thought. Law school was one way of proving to myself that I was a worthwhile person. I had to accomplish. It was vital to my existence—on drugs or off. On drugs, I could tolerate only perfection.

Graduation day arrived. It was hot. My blood pressure was abnormally high, so the sweat oozed from my pores in beads of sticky salt. I didn't want to be uncomfortable, so I wore my bikini under the opaque graduation gown.

When Papa asked me to pose for pictures, I was cranky and exhausted. There had been no opportunity to grab a pill, and I was beginning to slow down. Chris suggested that we have an early dinner so that I could get some rest. But instead of going to bed, I took an extra pill and stayed up most of the night packing. We left for Syracuse, New York, the next day. I kissed Vivian and Nat goodbye and promised to keep in touch. I never did.

I hopped into the back seat of the car amid the luggage, curled up, and went to sleep on the way home. I only woke up to stop on the New York State Thruway to go to the bathroom. The fifteen cups of coffee that I drank each day, combined with the pills, so aggravated my system that I had to stop every two hours. While I was in the ladies' room, I took some more pills. They did absolutely no good, but the effect was unimportant. Pill-taking had become a routine.

We arrived home six weeks before the wedding. Things were confused and hectic, but I liked them that way. The ceremony would take place in a big church—a Methodist church. Chris was a Baptist and I was a Roman Catholic. I had balked at the Catholic interpretation of marriage. I never believed that its sole purpose was simply to bear legitimate children.

The reception was to be held at the country club. My wedding advisor was an old friend of Mom's, in whom the proprieties of a socially elite wedding were very well ingrained. But I didn't give a damn about what society thought. I never have. She had arranged for a big ten-piece band and had selected stale dreary society music. I nipped the whole idea in the bud. At my wedding, I would have the musicians I wanted. I selected a Hungarian polka player whom Chris and I had heard in some offbeat restaurant. He played everything. I didn't want to fox trot even if it was hot. I wanted to waltz, rhumba, polka—I wanted to live.

As the days went by, I found little reason to stay off pills. The excitement of the wedding was rising. I was well stocked with prescriptions for the first trip to Connecticut. Chris was stationed there and had two more years of active duty service in the navy. While he was out at sea, I would return home and stay with Mom and Papa. I planned to take the New York State bar exam, continue working, and get through the ordeal with my teeth during Chris's first trip out.

Eventually, we'd settle in Syracuse; I'd practice law, and Chris would work for one of the big companies in the area. It made sense, since all my ties were Syracuse-based. So our life in Connecticut was temporary.

Chris arrived at the big house glowing with the excitement of a six-year-old on Christmas Eve. His copper-red hair sparked out from under the white O-cap, complemented by a stubborn cowlick that popped up every time the cap was removed. His clear complexion and rosy cheeks, which were dotted with freckles, gave the impression of a country boy who had been raised on whole milk, fresh eggs, and butter. Only his clear green eyes, tempered by long hours of work and study, showed the passing of twenty-four years. We talked briefly about remaining plans and then attended the wedding rehearsal.

I was married on August 1, 1967, at eleven o'clock in the morning. I had six bridesmaids, matching ushers, a maid of honor, and a flower girl. Although the temperature rose to 105 degrees, I felt nothing. I took four pep pills that morning and prepared ahead by stuffing six pills in my bra. My suitcase was loaded with two hundred pills and thirty blank prescriptions.

The music began. I had purposely selected something other than the Wedding March, since I hated all the jokes that were associated with it. I told Mom that I preferred "When the Saints Go Marching In," since it was more suited to the occasion. Again, I was "making an Eda"—something unusual, daring, and out of the ordinary. We settled for something more conservative. Later on, I would insist on having my own way.

I walked down the aisle slowly and deliberately, smiling at everyone in a blurred stare. When I arrived at the altar, I wasn't aware of Papa who stood behind me. I recited the marriage vows loudly and in my best diction. Then Papa was asked to give me away. At first he was speechless. Then I finally heard a meek voice, forced and crippled by tears, saying, "Mother and I give away Eda, our last daughter." My eyes glistened and a big lump formed in my throat. The soloist began singing the "Our Father." Her voice soared in soft strong tones among the high beams and stained-glass windows, leaving an ether of reverence over the scene below. Tears began streaming down my cheeks. Did I really know what I was doing? Why was Papa crying? I made every effort to hold back the heaving sighs that beat against my throat, aching and begging for release. Was I Chris's wife, or just Papa's little girl?

The ceremony ended with joyous music. With a tear-stained face, I put my arm in Chris's, and we were off to the reception—my party.

By bad planning, the reception line had been arranged in the afternoon sun. By then the temperature had risen to 110 degrees. I began to sweat but never felt the heat. The effect of the pills was holding up, and I still had the energy of a cross-country ski buff. I ate little and ordered a champagne glass filled with German beer. I wanted to dance. Despite the intense heat, I danced ten polkas. I adjourned to the ladies' room, took two more pills out of my bra, which I swallowed dry, and went out to dance some more. When Chris sat down, I danced with Papa. Although he was in his sixties, Papa never sat down when there was music playing.

By three o'clock, I noticed that the crowd had thinned out. Mom hinted that perhaps I should change my clothes. I was disappointed that I was expected to leave so soon. There was plenty of music left. Reluctantly, I changed my clothes and made a quick exit. We drove to a hotel about fifteen minutes away for our short honeymoon. Service leave didn't take honeymoons into account.

We arrived at the hotel and checked in. It was still hot. We unpacked, had a few drinks and dinner, and went to sleep. I was exhausted and slept most of the following day. I couldn't be totally off pills because I knew what was coming. I had to be in a happy mood. I knew that Chris was gentle, but I was afraid of intercourse in general. Chris was even more than gentle. In our dating days he had taken me out on Sunday mornings behind the Engineering Building to teach me how to French kiss.

But I wasn't ready for anything yet. Chris read *The Sunday New York Times* cover to cover during the first day while I slept and protested that I was exhausted. He read the *Ladies' Home Journal*, *The Saturday Evening Post,* and the *Sunday Chicago Tribune* while I slept the second day and protested that I was exhausted. The third day he read *Playboy* and anything else he could get his hands on. Finally, when he could read no more and wait no longer, he approached me. I loved him but was afraid. By placing his tongue in my vagina he brought me so close to orgasm that intercourse was inevitable. I was surprised that I hadn't felt any pain on penetration. I was relaxed. I kept wanting to try this new sensation again. I liked it. Since Chris was always controlled and got out in time, I was relieved of a greater fear than pain: pregnancy.

The next morning I was sore but less afraid. And I was confident that through Chris's artful lovemaking, I would also climax. Our relationship was different than most of the ones the marriage books described. I wasn't afraid to walk around in the nude. And, in the afternoon, after lunch by the pool, I would return to our room for my afternoon show. Turning on the radio, I'd start to strip, mimicking the professionals from the nightclubs in Florida. A wife should make love like a mistress, and I was learning fast. Whenever Chris wanted to make love, I grabbed him, tore off his clothes, and went to it like a playful kitten who's just discovered catnip.

Chris's leave was almost up, so we packed and drove to Connecticut with many stops along the way. My excuse was that I had to go to the ladies' room. Chris didn't know that I carried the pills in the lining of my purse and popped two at every stop.

When we arrived at the apartment, I started to unpack. Chris helped, but was required to spend a lot of time down at the ship. I took a few pep pills and happily approached what most people considered an ordeal. Unpacking was a task that could be measured. We had thirty boxes and I unpacked in twenty-four hours. I was taking thirty pills a day and moved with the speed of a Keystone Cops' chase in the silent flicks. I arranged everything in my own fashion. Chris thought I was intensely creative and imaginative. He said that only an "Eda" could have decorated the apartment in such an unusual and inexpensive way. Step by step, the apartment became a vivid reflection of my overactive mind.

I bought a rope hammock for five dollars that hung in one corner like a conch shell. Whenever company came, I immediately dumped all of my newspapers and magazines into the hammock. The hammock separated the living room from the dining room. To further separate the two living areas, I placed a Japanese screen behind the hammock. It was plain on one side and gilded with a Japanese landscape on the other.

The dining room lamp had presented a problem. It hung from the center of the ceiling—heavily gilded, ugly, and not appropriate, considering my Far Eastern decor. I would have replaced it with a stained-glass Tiffany, but buying expensive pieces was out of line with the challenge of creating an imaginative imitation out of material at hand. I bought a few pieces of purple felt, sewed them together, added a fancy fringe, and covered up the top of the lampshade. Then, from the inside, I hung a paper "Tiffany" upside down so that the light would be diffused rather than direct. To give my lamp an Oriental look, I hung thin gauze scarves from the handle on the bottom and scented them with my Shalimar perfume. At night my dining room passed for some offbeat bar in Algiers.

The living room was bare when I started. I had one wicker basket chair, a few Japanese cushions, and a large, ugly television set. I started by covering up the television set with a six-foot-diameter umbrella that I picked up for four dollars at the local five-and-ten. Whenever I had junk lying around, everything went under the Japanese umbrella. It had big red polka dots and was a good conversation starter.

I hated the venetian blinds on the windows and decided to leave them up all the time and paint the windows with tempera. Why not? I had studied art in Syracuse and won several of the scholastic key awards for my paintings while in high school. I bought some paint at the five-and-ten and went to work. It was unusual to paint on glass. The paintings were lit up by the morning sun and complemented in the afternoon by all the shades of twilight. The neighbors admired the reverse effect at night when the paintings were aglow from the indirect lights in my living room. There were Japanese landscapes done in blues and greens on one window and orange and yellows on the opposite window. Why hang a sheet or use the venetian blinds like everyone else? It was so much more fun to be creative. I'd erase and change my paintings every season!

The more pills I took, the more I became fascinated with light. God was out there in that sun, and I'd make a lamp for my living room that challenged the sparkle of a sunrise over Arctic waters. I popped some pills and set to work mounting a light bulb on a low stand. I then took a yellow wicker wastebasket, turned it upside down, and placed it over the mounted bulb. The top of the wastebasket served as an end table. On top of the wastebasket, I placed a large, round, hand-cut crystal dish. When I turned on the bulb, rays of light reflected through the small holes in the wastebasket, hit the crystal dish, and flashed a diamond-studded rainbow on the side wall. Four years later, I saw an expensive adaptation of my refractive lamp and wondered if the pills had merely distorted my reasoning ability, leaving my creative powers intact.

Encouraged by the compliments of visitors, I moved onto the remaining projects. I assembled my kite collection. I had a passion for all kinds of kites and loved to fly them in the fall. I collected half a dozen of various shapes, colors, and sizes. I hung a box kite in the hallway between the living room and the bathroom. I hung a handmade German kite in the shape of a bird on the side wall in the living room and a plain triangle kite from the ceiling in the living room. Whenever I wanted to fly, my kites were assembled.

The bathroom left little for my imagination. I neatly placed a kaleidoscope on top of the toilet just in case guests had nothing to do and wanted to look at it. Again, it was a conversation piece. For the men, I hung a *Playboy* calendar near the mirror.

I started in the kitchen with the ceiling lamps. I mounted my footstool and painted a happy face on the white globe in the middle of the room. On the globe above the sink where I washed dishes, I painted a sourpuss. There was no reason for this since my method of washing dishes was painless. I filled a bucket with Mr. Clean and dumped the dishes in to soak. Chris disapproved, but I insisted that my way was easier and more practical.

The linen closet in the living room was a good prospect for a bookcase—my last project. It had sliding doors and shelves on one side. I left one of the doors open and put all my books on the shelves. Chris came home and saw my newest creation.

"But, Eda, where are you going to put the sheets and towels?"

"I'll find someplace, honey, don't worry about it. Maybe I can fit them under the bed."

My initial spree at decorating was over. I was proud to have so much decoration for so little money. Children loved to visit my apartment. Adults found it unusual. One girl friend that I had made among the navy wives even asked me over to help decorate her new apartment. But, the more pep pills I took, the more my attention turned to details. I regularly polished pieces of copper, whether they needed it or not. I had an inlaid copper napkin ring that a friend of Mom's had given me a few years before. It bore the figure of a Chinese dragon. As I became more and more involved in my own peculiar world of fantasy, the more the ring became magic and of special significance.

Chris was gone most of the day, so he had no idea of what I was doing when alone. I established my prescriptions at the local drugstores and constantly went down for refills. One druggist noticed that I wasn't overweight, so I said that my metabolism was extremely low, and I needed the pills to keep active. He bought the story. I lied so many times that the story now came automatically and convincingly. I felt sick every time that I told it, but getting the pills made things all right again.

In the meantime, I started to read legal articles in *The New York Times* to review for the bar exam. I also watched television constantly and took special interest in the news. I'd serve dinner in front of the television set so that I could hear Walter Cronkite and Eric Sevareid. As I upped my dosage to thirty-five pills a day, I began to follow certain news stories. Congressman Adam Clayton Powell was up for censure. I felt that Powell was wrong and became obsessed with writing to Sevareid about it.

Before taking the big step of writing to Sevareid, I read all that I could about Powell. Instead of keeping up with my law studies, I bought every newspaper I could get my hands on and followed Powell's activities daily. Chris began to harp on reviewing for the bar exam. He was beginning to see a different Eda. I was enthusiastic and independent, but at times I would become fitful—downright nasty. When Chris disagreed with me on apartment decor, I insisted on my own way. I cited the favorable comments of friends on how unusual the place was. When we discussed Powell, I said what I thought—right or wrong—and quoted enough newspaper articles to make it sound like I knew my subject. I was right on matters that required rote memory and wrong on matters that required analysis.

Chris also noticed that I was good at small talk, although I somehow managed to monopolize the conversation. I had to succeed in making a good impression. I attended all the ladies' functions at the Officers' Club and was always alive, vibrant, and the last to leave. I wore the best of clothes and thought a lot of myself. I had built an image. The Eda on pills that I still remember was a daring, not-to-be-defeated, confident individual. Eda was passionate toward her mate, impetuous, but indifferent when his eyes turned to other women. It took a lot of confidence and absolutely no emotion. When I departed for Syracuse and Chris started seeing Eva Morgan, I had no objections; I thought that he should keep himself entertained while I was away. If he tried the same thing today, I'd string him up by the gonads.

After two months, I was running out of prescriptions. Pills and the pressure of the bar exam put the possibility of any unfaithfulness on the part of Chris out of my mind. He was going out to sea, and I planned to stay in Syracuse with Aunt Gabriella in her apartment at Papa's office.

The trip to Syracuse was uneventful. I took enough pills so that I wouldn't waste time eating. There would be plenty to eat at Aunt Gabriella's. She was one of the reasons I hated the thought of eating. Papa had been after her to go on a diet, but Papa was one to do a lot of talking. Since I had now found a way out, I never cared about Papa's silly routine of eating too much, announcing weight gain, and resolving to start a diet the next day. I had listened to this for some twenty-odd years. Later, when I came off amphetamines, the concern about weight became an obsession that I have never conquered.

When I arrived, Aunt Gabriella had prepared a "light" supper; salad, chicken, pasta, bread, wine, and dessert. We had little to talk about, but she was impressed that I was going to be a professional like her brother. I would follow in Papa's footsteps.

Later the conversation turned to damning the rest of the family. Roy, who had married my sister Angelina, was a no-good bum. He had done a lot for Gabriella, but she wasn't convinced that he was good enough for Angelina in the first place. Henry, who had married my older sister Stella, was cruel because he wouldn't allow Papa to see the grandchildren. My brother Luciano was a pacifist. So he was out too—according to my aunt. My youngest brother, Rocco, offered promise. He should go on to medical school and be a professional. Then he would be a success.

Her opinions had a profound effect on Papa. Gabriella took precedence over Mom and exercised an unnatural influence over her brother. Since she lived at the office, she had a lot of time to talk to Papa. She spoiled him to death. Despite our differences, she and I got along together the first few days. I was down at the law office most of the time trying to show Ralph, my boss, that I could work during the day, review for the bar exam at night, and go to the dentist's whenever I had to. He looked at me and smiled: "Eda, you'll have no trouble passing. I've never known a girl that was such a tiger and ate up law so much. Slow down and take it easy. It will be a long haul."

I was egged on by his encouraging words. I convinced myself that what everyone told me was right. It was easier than thinking and less destructive.

Next, I went to the dentist. Dr. Giddons told me that a complete tooth-by-tooth restoration was necessary. I was on my second set of caps and had gone through the agony of braces at twenty-one. The next appointment was scheduled for the following week. Giddons wanted complete X-rays. After that, I was scheduled for three-hour periods three times a week. I popped a few pills when I heard the news—which only served to aggravate the pain that I constantly felt in my teeth at that time. Giddons hoped the whole thing would last three months. He scheduled the final fitting for two days before the bar exam. I was upset that the dental work would interfere with studying and discouraged that I had to waste so much time on good health and vanity. Vanity had no bearing on being a top-notch lawyer. Passing the bar was the most important thing in my life. It meant success and good standing in the eyes of my family.

Next, I made half-baked plans for taking the bar review course. The review was given three hours a night at a local office building near my place of work.

Right away, Aunt Gabriella was disappointed that I had no time to visit or take her downtown shopping. She wanted me to relax. I didn't know what the word meant. When I was at her apartment, I was studying, writing, or watching the news on television. Though there was always the pressure to socialize with all of the Franchi relatives, I was adamant. When relatives called, I gave the excuse that I was going through an intensive review for the bar exam and couldn't take the time off. Everyone felt sorry and warned me against studying too hard. I had a reputation, on and off drugs, for overdoing things.

The bar review course started the same time as the dental work. I paid my visit to Giddons at nine on a Monday morning. I decided right away that I was going to like Dr. Giddons. He liked me. I was bright and, in the painful days that followed, I proved to be courageous. No one could figure out why I stayed so optimistic despite the ordeal that awaited me.

Dr. Giddons and I chatted while he made molds of my teeth. When he wasn't busy working on my mouth, we would chat some more and take a cigarette break. Although seventy years old, he started work at seven every morning and stayed until five in the afternoon. He was fascinated by the bad work that had been done on my teeth and considered total restoration a personal challenge. He would work for three hours at a time and then let me go for a day to let my gums heal from the Novocain shots. As the work went deeper into my gums, I needed ten to twelve shots at one sitting to quell the pain.

The work of removing each nerve and scraping down my gums was tedious and nauseating. I stayed on a high dosage of pills.

When I got back to Aunt Gabriella's apartment from work or the dentist's, I allowed no time to get adjusted to the routine. I'd gobble down dinner, excuse myself, and get lost for an hour with my books in Papa's office before taking off to the bar review. I tried to prepare for the next lecture rather than review. I was beginning to feel the pressure of time.

I entered the first three-hour session of the bar review with high hopes. Most of the students were married and working to support families. They had a lot riding on the exam, and some were afraid of flunking. I had never been told that I would flunk, and because of my pills, I was beyond feeling fear, or any emotion.

But I had no right to be confident about passing. I had received the material weeks in advance and still hadn't touched it. I sensed that this bar exam might be overwhelming, yet I listened to those who said I had always worked too hard. Following their advice was easier than thinking for myself.

At the sessions, I took copious notes which I never reread. I'd pop a few pills and tell myself that I would worry about reviewing later. When I complained to Ralph at work that the bar review was nerve-shattering, he smiled: "Eda, you'll make it. Have a little confidence in yourself, honey. When you pass, you'll be the best-looking lady lawyer in Syracuse."

I had pages and pages of review notes to cover and little reasoning power left. I'd learn one principle of law and rely on it to solve any problem—no matter how remote and tortured the connection. Now I see this. At the time I was on pills, I didn't. I was convinced that I knew law as well as the next person. It was just a matter of becoming fully aware of all the principles involved. Even at work, Ralph often remarked on how thoroughly

I handled a case. He never stopped to think that I was too thorough.

Slowly, and toward the end of my employment, I indulged in another old and dangerous habit which killed my chances of passing the bar. I continued reading about the Powell investigation. No one knew that I was devoting half a day to reading *The Times* and getting behind on my legal work. I became more involved with current events like the Vietnam war. I read the editorials, especially those by James Reston, Tom Wicker, and Arthur Sulzberger. Everyone thought that reading *The Times* was advisable. Ralph bought it daily and often gave me a copy. But I wasn't reading *The Times* to merely keep abreast of the news; I was going to do something about what was going on.

One month before the bar review was over, I felt work was getting to be too much of a burden. I was now taking off three afternoons a week to go to the dentist's. The pain from the dental work increased. So on a Friday morning, I went in to see Ralph and explained the situation. He understood and asked that I keep in touch. Now my life involved only two things: the bar review and the new set of teeth.

The trips to the dentist were enjoyable only because of Dr. Giddons. I looked forward to talking about my plans in law as well as my tastes in music, hobbies, and sports. When I wasn't talking—which wasn't very often—he would tell me about his trips to the Far East.

The dental work was becoming complicated by the number of pills that I took. Giddons commented on how tight my jaw always was and how the muscles in my face never relaxed. I'd casually smile and answer, "Why, Doctor, how would you feel if you saw that drill coming at you and didn't know if the Novocain would work? Just the smell of so much blood and pus nauseates me. I come here only because you have such a charming personality. Segovia's music is so much more interesting than a lousy mess of teeth."

Giddons was then giving me eight to ten shots of Novocain a day. When I began to shake, I didn't know whether it was the amphetamines or the after-effects of the Novocain. He had asked me if I was taking any other medication; I had lied and told him no. Novocain would only affect my mouth and not my nervous system, so it was inconsequential that I was also taking amphetamines. To complicate matters, I was also on a dosage of codeine to relieve the pain from the dental work. My gums had swollen from the many Novocain shots, and they smoldered with pain every time I ate or drank. I took the codeine that Giddons prescribed only when the tears were streaming down my cheeks, and I could no longer talk or eat. After each trip to the dentist's, I'd come home panting, stomp on the floor with my feet, raise my hands to my face in agony, and march around grunting to relieve the pain. Finally, the codeine took effect. This was the choice that I had made to stay active, alert, and happy.

I managed to attend all the sessions of the bar review course. But deep down, I couldn't escape the fact that I was basically unprepared. I had made no plans to go to Buffalo to take the exam. Subconsciously, I started to look for an excuse. It had to be a good one; one that I could hold up in front of the world that I knew and avoid looking like a coward. When Giddons scheduled my major fitting on the day of the bar exam, I was elated. No one could have convinced me that I was avoiding a test of fear—fear of failure.

My study mates at the bar review didn't understand why I continued with the course when I didn't intend to take the exam. Ralph said that the dental work was too much when combined with the bar review. I exaggerated the story of the fitting and told everyone that I would have to go to the hospital. Eda had to look good and Eda had to be right. I souped up the story to fit my taste and satisfy my audience. The pain from the dental work was my own doing, the result of amphetamines, so I had no qualms about fudging. Me. The suffering heroine.

My relationship with Aunt Gabriella was becoming unbearable. I was jumpy about my decision not to take the bar exam, and her habits had begun to grate on my nerves. My stomach was in a constant state of flux due to the Novocain or the amphetamines. The slightest unpleasantness made me vomit. Aunt Gabriella was heavy, and she had a strong odor. I had mentioned it to her when she asked me why I vomited in the morning after breakfast. How could anyone eat a decent meal when they had to sit opposite such a stench. I decided to move back to the big house on the lake and stay alone. Mom and Papa were still in Egypt, so their fourteen-room house was unoccupied.

I telephoned Mrs. Yates, our next-door neighbor, and asked to sleep at her place across the street, since I was afraid of being by myself at night. But during the day I wanted to be alone. I found people—especially my relatives—too demanding about the amount of time I was required to spend with them. The Yateses were different. Mrs. Yates let me come and go as I pleased—no questions asked.

I moved to the big house in short order, promising Aunt Gabriella that I would visit her in the future and that things were better this way. My teeth were still bothering me and I needed the rest. I took a few pills when I arrived in order to get settled and avoid feeling lonesome. Then, after unpacking, I went over to see Mrs. Yates.

My days at the big house on the lake were uneventful. I stayed close to the Yates place and enjoyed many an evening talking about my future plans with Mrs. Yates. Physically, I was improving. I no longer vomited and I began to eat. But during the remaining time that I spent in Syracuse, I was homesick for my man. I tried to take enough pills to keep me busy, but I couldn't obliterate the feeling. I devoted most of my time to the bar review course. Now that the pressure was off and I had saved face by using the dentist as an excuse, I attended the sessions with more confidence and decided I would compile enough notes so that I could comfortably review on my own in Connecticut with Chris.

I was also in constant pain, with only two weeks of dental care to go. I'd march through the rooms of the big house, pounding the doors with my fists and panting from the incessant aching in my teeth. To quell the pain, I took codeine. To pep up, I took amphetamines. To put myself to sleep at night, I took phenobarbital, Deprol, or any other barbiturate samples that I found floating around the big house. I couldn't live without any one of these pills. The codeine and the barbiturates made me dopey, so I had to up the dosage of amphetamines. The sedatives assured me a good night's sleep without the recurrence of any "frozen dreams." I was constantly floating until I got zipped up—until I got doped up. I didn't have to think, and basically I was very happy. People who questioned me raised ugly issues of my future. I couldn't afford to change because I didn't know where to start. If I went off amphetamines, I would sleep for days and then my personality would start to switch. How it would change, I didn't know. I was in a bind and too proud to tell Chris what I was really like. The present was more acceptable than the unknown. A combination of amphetamines and barbiturates was safe. One kept me happy, and the other kept me sane. That was all I wanted out of life, besides success.

When the big day of the bar exam arrived, I went to Dr. Giddons' office for the last and messiest part—the fittings. They took about three hours. I was soon back at the big house, packed and bidding good-bye to Mrs. Yates. I also stopped to say farewell to Aunt Gabriella and, while there, picked up a whole pad of prescriptions. Chris was in port and waiting for me.

I pushed eighty miles an hour on the thruway and arrived in Connecticut in one piece. Chris opened the door, grabbed me in one swoop, and gave me a long kiss. I regained my breath and looked around. The house was a mess as I expected, but it made no difference. I was home.

Chris wanted to have dinner at home. I was tired and didn't want to miss Walter Cronkite and Eric Sevareid on the evening news. We brought in our dinner trays, and then the phone rang. A girl's voice asked for Chris. He talked for about fifteen minutes and then came back to watch television.

"Who was that?" I asked casually.

"Eva Morgan."

"Who's Eva Morgan? If it involves a long discussion, save it until after the news. I've got to follow up on this Adam Clayton Powell character. Chris, he's so wrong. Something has to be done about him before he goes any further. I'm tempted to write Eric Sevareid and give him a piece of my mind."

"Don't you want to know who Eva Morgan is?"

"Your girl friend while I was away."

"How did you know?"

"It didn't sound like your mother."

"You don't mind?"

"How can I mind? I don't know if she's pretty—or smart—or what plans she has for you."

"Then you're not mad?"

"Why should I be? As long as you don't get her into trouble and take her out only when I'm out of town, I don't care."

"We just started out being friends."

"Did you go to bed with her?"

"Yes."

"Then she thinks you're more than just friends."

"That's not what she said."

"I know that's not what she said, my dear, but I hope you don't believe everything that a single girl tells you—or is she married?"

"No, she's not married."

"Does she know that you're married?"

"No."

"Do you plan to tell her?"

"That's what I wanted to ask you. What should I do?"

"That's up to you."

"I don't want to hurt her. I like her."

"Do you love her?"

"No. And now that you're back, Eda, I don't want her. I missed you so much while you were away, I just sought her companionship. I was friends with you for five years, and I didn't see that things would be different with anyone else."

"If you don't want her, tell her that you're married. She'll be more hurt if you lead her on. If you want to keep her as a friend, start out by telling her the truth. You'll probably get a good bawling-out, which you damn well deserve. At least she has a more informed choice when she goes to bed with you. Invite her over when I go back to Syracuse, and put the whole thing to her straight. If I were in her position, I'd give you a damned hard time."

Chris interrupted the talk to get a drink. In the meantime, I popped a pill. If the whole affair wasn't ironed out that night, he probably wouldn't sleep.

"Eda, I'm going to be good to you. I'm going to abstain and tell all other women to leave me alone."

"Hogwash. I don't object to your running around with other girls while I'm away—just as long as I know the score. You were unfair and acted like a moron in this case. When a girl says she wants to be friends, she's looking for a husband."

"You weren't."

"Never mind. I'm different. I didn't go to bed with you either. I'll bet this poor girl is in love with you. If she is, that's the end of a beautiful friendship. This isn't the first time that I've had to advise you on how to get uninvolved with another woman. It probably won't be the last. By the way—what are all those prints doing on the wall?"

"Eva said the same thing. She thought the apartment was so imaginatively decorated. But she felt that the prints didn't belong. I hung them there after you left."

"I'd like to meet Eva sometime. She sounds interesting. If you're going to have a mistress, I ought to at least approve of her."

"You're kidding!"

"No, I'm not. It's only natural for a man to crave sex while his wife is away. As long as Eva doesn't make a fool out of herself and get pregnant, I don't care."

And with an "Eda, I love you," Chris went to bed. I stayed up and watched the late show. The intense emotional pain of being rejected for another woman never penetrated my senses. Pills assured me the detached approach of overconfident reasoning. If Chris preferred Eva Morgan to me, then he wasn't worth it in the first place. Why should I fear my competition? My pill didn't wear off until early morning, and I didn't feel the need for a sleeping pill.

The next day Chris went down to the ship as usual. I stayed around the house attempting to clean it from the bottom up. We forgot about Eva Morgan until the next week when she called again. When Chris hung up the phone, we had another short chat. Chris had met her parents.

"Don't you know that bringing the beau home means that she has plans for you?"

"No."

"Well, I didn't bring you home to Syracuse to meet my relatives until we were practically engaged. What do you and Eva talk about?"

"Many things. She thinks a lot like you as far as women's career plans. She holds a responsible position at IBM."

"What does she look like?"

"Well, she's not as good-looking as you. She's long and tall."

"Does she have any other boy friends?"

"I don't know."

"Well, this is the second week in a row, so I suggest you have her over for a talk. I'll go over and see Bonnie next door. For her sake, you ought to get things straight. That is, if you want to. You've got to watch out, Chris. You're the type that appeals to women. You look so young and boyish. Since you're basically not out for sex in the first place, it's much easier to get what you want. Don't buy the story that every girl wants to become friends. Unless they're afraid of the stagnation that usually ensues with marriage, they'll throw career, success, and everything down the drain once they find a man."

"You didn't."

"I didn't want to get married in the first place. But it

was the only ethical thing to do since you wanted sex as well as companionship. If Eva Morgan wants a career, she's not going about it in the right way."

"Okay, I'll tell her on your next trip to Syracuse."

"That's your business. In the meantime, I want to watch Walter Cronkite and Eric Sevareid. I'm tempted to write them about the Powell situation. They shouldn't let him into Congress."

"Eda, I wish you wouldn't. You should start reviewing for the bar exam."

"I will. But the exam isn't given until March, and this is intimately connected with my review. It's a matter of law."

And write I did. My letter to Sevareid was three pages long, handwritten, and the beginning of hundreds of letters that I was to write on all aspects of the news. None of the letters made any sense. I started writing about the injustice of the Powell situation and ended up with the war in Vietnam.

In order to impress Sevareid, I used flowery paper— parchment. To make my letters more attractive, I went down to the post office to buy the newest variety of stamps. Again it was an "Eda." Chris read one of the letters, and we had a fight. I thought that my letters were carefully read and every broadcast after that was an immediate response to my letter of the previous week. Since the commentary and the subject of my letter usually coincided, Chris was never able to convince me that they were designated as "crackpot" letters by the network mail clerk.

The more pills I took, the more I was convinced of my own powers. I was the unseen influence behind Sevareid's response to world questions. If it wasn't reality—if it wasn't the truth—I wasn't concerned. I had now graduated to a world of my own. I was slowly becoming omnipotent.

Omnipotence was the surge of power in my own beliefs. It kept me hooked. After four pep pills in the morning, I was anxious to get things accomplished. I was immensely happy and enthusiastic. Not a day would pass that I didn't come up with an "Eda": something unexpected, something exciting, something that demanded the immediate admiration of my husband Chris. And if something was not done my way, I just took a few more pills to happily adjust to the new situation. I now averaged thirty-five to forty Preludin, or roughly 1,000 milligrams a day.

There was importance and meaning in everything that I did. Even though I avoided realities like the bar exam, I was free from the normal feelings of failure and guilt. At home, I started with physical accomplishments. I could show Chris that I cleaned up the house, cooked something new, or changed the décor. I rearranged the furniture every day and added something new. Chris was never sure that he was walking into the same place. I'd spend hours at the supermarket or at different stores picking up things that I didn't need but felt would decorate my home.

Soon, I devoted most of the day to enlightened analyses of what I read in the news or saw on television. I wrote to Eric Sevareid, Walter Cronkite, James Reston, Tom Wicker, Arthur Sulzberger, and Rod Serling once or twice a day. I digested three to five newspapers a day—including a cover-to-cover review of *The New York Times*. I started clipping out copies of the editorials that I wanted to comment on, and I forecast that someday my letters might be published in the "Letters to the Editor" column. The importance of my reading was to do something about the news and get a reaction. Chris disagreed with this but felt that my efforts were harmless as long as I devoted some time to reviewing for the bar.

I had fixed plans regarding Adam Clayton Powell. If the man played his cards right, he could become a hero. I quickly addressed a letter to him and sent it to a man who had connections with him. It read:

Dear Adam Powell:
You're too smart a jet to get locked out by your cohorts in Congress whose consciences are colored blacker than your deeds. Heed my advice and come out of this smelling like fresh brewed coffee instead

of a Georgia swamp. Disclose to the public all the other bribes, deals, payoffs, and scandals that you know about in Congress. By comparison, you'll look good. Pay off the widow in the libel suit. You'll be a hero rather than a left-out mutt . . .

At the same time, I wrote to the Supreme Court of New York, advising them of the potential bad effects of their decision in favor of Powell's congressional immunity from suit. With my letter, I included a copy of *Games People Play* by Eric Berne and suggested they read it. Somehow I connected it with the Powell incident. I remember reading in *The Times* that one of the Supreme Court justices referred to the game of "cops and robbers"; since this game was mentioned in the book, I reasoned that my letter had some effect.

My letter writing took up all of the afternoon and most of the night. I had no obligations to meet and never got bored. Slowly, however, in the course of months, Chris saw changes. I began to get sharp and jumpy. Chris would make arrangements to go to a navy party. I didn't want to go. I wanted to write letters. I insisted on watching television; he wanted to be with other people. I had to plan my trips to the druggist, so I was angry when he showed up unexpectedly. I didn't want him to find me out and yet felt guilty that I should keep so great a sin from the man I loved.

At times I tried to make this up to Chris. I was always around but had to be in the specific mood for spur-of-the-moment activities. I would take three or four pills whenever we went to a party. When I got crabby, I'd go into the bathroom, take a few pills out of my bra, and get back on an even level.

At this time, I was a light drinker. Alcohol brought me down. After a beer, I would usually excuse myself, go into the bathroom, and nullify the effects by taking a few more pills.

Once I started on a continual overdose, I became sexually overactive. I was always interested in having intercourse. When Chris came home in the afternoon, I was hot. I wanted nothing but the most active foreplay. I went wild when he bit my tits and I told him to bite harder. After the first climax, I was exhausted but willing to go for another two or three rounds. When Chris wasn't home, I would lie stomach down on the bed, imagine the most erotic thing I could, and masturbate. I'd picture a bunch of cowboys stopping a stagecoach, lifting up a woman's fluffy skirts and playing with her vagina, each taking his turn while everyone else looked on. It was important that everyone else watched. While they were watching and doing nothing despite her screams, I would usually reach orgasm. The whole thing took a matter of five minutes and left me unsatisfied. I'd quiver from the first orgasm and want to do it again.

At times, I was completely frustrated. Chris's timing was off or I got too excited. I couldn't bear the feeling of frustration. I'd writhe on the bed and almost vomit from lack of satisfaction. It didn't happen very often, but when it did, I was in tears, beating the bedsheets.

Chris was surprised that I was so active sexually. My increased sexuality deluded me into thinking that the main part of our marriage was sexual compatibility. Since I was so new at sex, had learned it so fast, and was so interested in all of its ramifications, I couldn't stop. The marriage books said that I should be passive and accommodate. Hell. I wanted to arouse and excite; I wanted passion. I had this power and enjoyed using it to its fullest. I read that so many wives had problems of modesty, shame, or abstention. I would be the opposite—the voluptuous she-wolf that my man wanted.

My concern about taking the bar exam diminished in favor of a basic hostility toward the inequity and injustice of a written exam. It meant conforming to other people's standards. A bar exam where all were questioned on the same old thing was no test of knowledge at all. I wrote to the Supreme Court of New York and told them that an oral appearance before the Board of Bar Examiners was the only real test. I abhorred the idea of standard answers to legal questions. I argued in my letter to each different justice that the court should adopt the practice used in European countries where the real test was thinking on your feet. My way was the right way. But I'd talk matters over with a friend before doing anything drastic.

Asa was a bad person to talk to. He was Arabian and more accustomed to foreign teaching. I could call him "Nat" or "Rex" from my college days because that's the kind of relationship that I had established. I met Asa in an unusual way. My parents sent me a camel saddle from Egypt that was broken on delivery. I wasn't prepared to let the matter go, so I contacted an Egyptian couple in the apartment complex and asked them if they knew anyone who could write Arabic. They gave me Asa's address. I called on him and asked him to write a letter in Arabic about the damage. We got to talking, and I found out that he had just graduated with a doctorate from the University of Wisconsin. He was overjoyed to find someone with a connection to his college days and refused any money for the translation. So I invited him over for dinner.

When a letter finally came back from Egypt, I called Asa over for a translation. The store owner would forward a camel saddle free of charge. Then I broached the question of the bar exam. I wanted discussion but no disagreement.

"Asa, you know how people study in Europe?"

"Yes, they take competitive oral exams."

"Here they don't. When I go to the bar exam, I will be expected to write the same stock phrases and answers that were expected of me in law school. I don't think it's fair. The whole point of being a lawyer is to advocate one position and argue all the law that you know. I don't want to decide."

"Eda, your plan sounds radical. It sounds right, but it sounds radical. If you return your ticket of admission to the bar examiners, then you won't be able to take the exam. You had to submit all those papers in order to get the ticket in the first place."

"That's not the point. I'm used to standing up for what

I believe in. If I'm going to believe in being a lawyer, I have to do it my way. Too many people are afraid of innovation, Asa—especially lawyers. They go through life like wilted lettuce—thinking nothing, folding under pressure, and complaining that the current situation is unjust. They won't risk anything to change it. I may be a fool, but I go to bed at night with a clear conscience."

"Eda, you talk so emphatically, maybe you can change things."

"Chris says that I should wait until I take the exam before I start to protest."

"It's up to you. Just don't offend those who believe that a written test is the only way of passing so many students. I admire you for your courage, Eda. The court might consider your proposal, even though they don't acknowledge your letters."

"Asa, recognition isn't important. If it's my place to exert influence, to hold power—although unrecognized—then I'm satisfied. When Chris says that my letters only embarrass him, I feel like a misdirected idiot. He tells me to take an interest in the news. But it's no good if all I'm going to do is discuss it at the next cocktail party."

"Return your ticket of admission to the bar examiners. Don't take it. I'm all for you, Eda."

I folded up my ticket with a covering letter requesting that I be given an oral exam. I never received a response. I wasn't sure that I had done the right thing, but I was beyond feeling guilt. I was reaching the point of total omnipotence, where I had influence over any endeavor that I undertook and I was always right.

Chris returned from a trip on the boat and found out that I had returned my ticket. He asked about my plans. I decided to take a vacation in Florida, where my parents were now staying. He felt that I needed a rest and agreed. This was his chance to square with Eva.

I made my reservations that day and my parents met me at the airport that night. As usual, they were delighted by my visit. I talked all the way back to their apartment. Then Papa posed the question of the bar exam. I was ill-prepared to defend my position and promised to discuss it with him the next day. In the meantime, I asked Mom how to break it to Papa. I felt Papa would object but I didn't care that much about his reaction. I was right.

Mom didn't agree with me but said: "Eda, we don't care if you become a lawyer. What matters is your happiness. Your father will be disappointed, but he thinks well of you no matter what you do."

"Mom, I'm tired of being pushed around by a bunch of people who don't think before they do something. I can't change my stand. I don't want to be a lawyer if it means less than living up to a particular standard of excellence. The time to act is now—not wait until after I passed the exam. They know how much is at stake. I can't suppress my individuality for the sake of a bunch of conforming fish. Papa will say that I'm wrong, but I don't give a damn. Lawyers talk about uniform laws, uniform codes, and yet they can't even get together and make up a national exam for their members. I'm not fed up with fighting. I'll even use my law in a more creative field—like advertising. Advertising, combined with law, could prove of great advantage."

"Eda, you're missing the point. If you've come this far, you might as well finish. I don't understand your logic. We'll talk it over with Papa in the morning."

I stayed awake that night wrestling with thoughts. Maybe I was slowly going crazy. No. Instead of me, the world was going through the phases of a nervous breakdown. No one gave a damn any more about the big, powerful issues. No one wanted to change the present. I popped another pill and thought some more. Did returning the ticket mean more than proving my cause? Sacrifice was part of any great cause. My anguish was worthwhile, as long as I could break with my chosen profession and make them eat crow. I'd go into advertising and slander the hell out of lawyers for their apathy toward change.

As I expected, Papa didn't understand why I returned my ticket to the bar exam. It was not a matter of principle at all. I refused to take the exam. If I didn't want to be a lawyer, that was one thing. If I wanted to make an ass out of myself, that was another. Papa didn't believe in causes

—not where becoming a professional was concerned. He urged me to take the exam again.

During the rest of our time at the beach, Mom and Papa were great company. We went to all the nightclubs and walked along miles of white, warm sand. There was always Mom to talk to. I thought of Mom as a sister—closer to me than Stella or Angelina—closer than anyone else I will ever know except Chris.

But it was time to leave Florida. I was running out of pills. I was slowing down and relaxing. I hadn't read the news for two weeks; I was beginning to feel that Chris might get out of line with Eva.

Part Two

I had no plans when I returned to Connecticut, but it made little difference. I had my causes. When I wasn't reading the newspapers or watching television, I was redecorating the house. I polished everything, including the Chinese napkin ring. When Chris said that I would polish the enamel off the ring, I retorted that it brought me good luck. Every morning that I polished the ring, my day started off well.

I expanded my interest in the news. The more I read, the more I felt a part of what I was reading. Soon, however, my thoughts became jumbled. My theories about the world were changing and also the things I said and did in relation to it. China was in the news a lot, and I became concerned when I saw them training three- and four-year-old children to fight. Mao was building an army such as we had never known. What had happened with Athens and Sparta could happen all over again with the United States and China.

I wrote a letter to Sevareid telling him that we weren't doing enough. We left China out of the United Nations. China would make us pay through the teeth for such an error. Why not take the wind out of their sails by treating them as a recognized power? I rubbed my napkin ring and thought that Eda Franchi Spaight ought to do something about this. I no longer believed in the reality of death, so there was no danger of being killed. I proposed a plan and asked Sevareid to forward a letter to Mao. I enclosed a check for $50 to cover the cost of translation into Chinese. The letter read:

Dear Chairman Mao,

Despite all the people in the United States that hate you, a common ground of understanding can be reached. I have admired your culture and possess only one relic from your civilization. I am willing to act as an unofficial representative from my country in order to show you that out of all those that you despise, one has some respect for your ways and wishes to accommodate your civilization. I wish to meet with your woman, and would gladly learn your language so that I can convince my people of your basic worth. Since I am not of your rank, I humbly ask you to send someone to the island of Sicily— time and place to be arranged at your convenience. I feel that it's wrong that you're not recognized in the United Nations and am willing to show you and your people that one—if only one—in the United States is willing to recognize your cause. When I meet with your chosen representative, I shall bring with me the relic of your civilization that may lead you to results in solving the heavy problems that rest on your shoulders—problems of war and a starving people. If you are a wise leader, you will heed my advice.

I never received an answer to my letter but recall a special visit by Chairman Mao. I awoke at five on a Sunday morning and heard a nightingale outside my window. She sang so sweetly. It was the story of the Emperor and the Nightingale in real life. I put on a dress and went outside in the wet morning dew to find the nightingale. I walked through the deserted lot in the back of the apartment house, making my way through the undergrowth, weeds, and stumps of uprooted trees. As I walked, I mumbled: "Mom, this isn't much of a garden—nothing like the one we had at home. No roses, no peonies, no poppies. It doesn't look like the Emperor's garden at all and yet I hear the nightingale so clearly."

I continued walking until the apartment house became a black silhouette against a muted curtain of dawn. I was now in the garden of Eden—what was left of the original after hundreds of years of abuse. I looked up at the moon, slowly yielding to the first rays of sunlight, and cried: "God, what have humans done to this earth but made a colossal ulcer out of it."

I started to skip. Mom would skip through the garden like this. She would jump as I jumped in my slippers. Tears came to my eyes as I whispered under my breath: "Oh, Mom. You had life right! One should never go through life without skipping, jumping and enjoying her garden."

Eventually Chris was up and looking for me. He came outside, dressed in his khakis—which was a mistake. For a few minutes, he was Chris, and then his face began to change. It widened and flattened. His skin turned yellow and his green eyes became two almonds. He became heavier and his hair was no longer red. It was black. I was confronted by the owner of my garden who had come in response to my letter. I no longer heard what Chris was saying; I heard the answers to my questions. The man seemed kind, and yet I was afraid of him. Chairman Mao, who then stood before me, trained killers.

Mao smiled and we sat down at a picnic table. I started:

"Do you think there is any hope for the world as long as my country continues to be so obstinate about recognizing you? It's embarrassing, especially when I have studied your people and your language out of nothing more than pure admiration. We're being unrealistic and impractical. It's always best to know your enemy better than he knows himself—at least that's been my theory of survival. Right or wrong, you are reality. Would you like the relic that you came for?"

I went in the apartment and when I returned with my dragon ring, Chris was sitting on the bench shaking his head.

"Eda, you were saying things that made no sense."

"I must have been dreaming. All I know is that I'm out here with my Turkish slippers all full of mud and holding a napkin ring. I remember something about Chairman Mao and a nightingale."

"Eda, you've said the same thing in your letters to Sevareid. Were you dreaming or were you saying what you actually thought?"

"I don't know. I only slept for an hour last night and I'm dead tired. Let's go back to sleep, honey."

That was the first time that I saw things that didn't actually exist and heard things that weren't said. I wasn't frightened by meeting Chairman Mao or having the world change for me. When I became depressed or preoccupied, I took my pep pills faithfully and thought that everything would soon be all right. I had now left the world of the living. Except for the lucid intervals, I was now in a world of my own.

Chris was gone during most of the day when I devoted my time to reading, answering the news items, and watching television. When Chris asked me what I intended to accomplish, I started to expound my new philosophy. What bothered Chris was my total conviction that I was right.

"Chris," I began, in a sermon that I was bound to lose, "in every society there's a need for thinkers. Most people today are only conscious of world events when those events influence their immediate sphere of living. The rest is left to the brains—the hired thinkers in Washington who really rule. Many countries have philosophers who do nothing but put a reason on the current trend of thought. You say that no one cares, but still, someone may have the guts to listen to what I advise and change the current course of disaster. If we would only tolerate Red China, they wouldn't act like a bunch of spoiled brats that were left out of the neighborhood crowd. They wouldn't decide that it's best to blast us off the face of the earth. One thing you can't do with such an intense hatred is ignore it."

"Eda, our government is in capable hands."

"Everyone says that. And then presto—you have a Hitler on your hands. Shit. They all got what they deserved. Don't ask for a better world and no one will do it for you. If I don't become involved with the things that are ultimately going to determine my future, I die. People go through life dying. They convince themselves that they're too old and then they rot. Look at this guy who has the auto companies at his feet. He started his own show. And that's what I'll do too, by God, if no one listens to me. I'll go to New York City and combine law with the more dynamic field of advertising. Because my ideas go unacknowledged, you say that they're worthless."

"Maybe you're right, Eda, and maybe you should use your ideas. But calm down first. Get settled here. You come here for a few weeks and then you're off again. I love you, Eda, and I want you with me. Together we can accomplish so much. I told Eva that. I have such high hopes for us, Eda. I can't see you wasting your life away in unnoticed commentary. You're overambitious. You should slow down enough to at least think things out."

"That's why I thought you loved me—because I am dynamic, because I am different, because I intend to make something out of my life."

"That's what you say, Eda. But then you spend the whole day in the house, watching television, writing letters, and talking about going down to New York or Washington. You don't visit Bonnie next door. You haven't called Asa in a month. Being with people is an important part of life. You get so wound up in what you're doing that you forget other people. Don't ever forget people, Eda. You need them."

After our discussion, I tried to vary my interests. I went out to the five-and-ten and bought more small things to decorate the house. When our friends invited us out, I took them up on it. But in the back of my mind, my ideas were growing like yeast. Every program that I watched on television had references to my letters.

Rod Serling and his program "Twilight Zone" was one of my favorites. His ads for a correspondence course in writing meant that he knew that I wanted to express something. It was time for more positive action. My visions of the universe were beginning to jell, and I experimented with tangible things to illustrate my theories. I wrote

Serling a letter expounding my new views. It was the last letter before my entrance into the hospital for a nervous breakdown:

> Dear Mr. Serling:
> Your recent program dealt with one man's drive to achieve excellence. It's difficult. One must view oneself from the inside out. Then only by bending back upon oneself can excellence be achieved. Because the concept is so difficult, I have enclosed the only symbol that I know of excellence. An unbroken circle, though never opened, can be twisted and shaped enough to bend and touch both extremities. Keep the jewel that I send you. I don't need it since I have found excellence and inner peace. I am a circle with no beginning and no end, yet twisted around and back upon myself such as this bracelet that I send you.

I folded the parchment letter, and placed it in a box with a solid gold bracelet that I had received as a wedding present. The clasp of the bracelet was mounted with star rubies and sapphires. I had twisted the strands of gold into a figure eight, closed the clasp, and mailed it off to Serling. The handmade piece would retail in this country for about $800. It was later returned with a note that Mr. Serling didn't accept such valuable gifts.

In the meantime, my ideas of combining law and advertising gave rise to a whole new vision of job opportunities. I read in *The Times* about Mary Wells who had made it to the top with her own firm. My imagination knew no bounds. I would go to New York and get a job—even a job without pay. I wrote to Mary Wells and told her that a combination of advertising and law would be worthwhile.

Then Chris saw the note from Serling. It was time for another talk. I found it more and more difficult to explain my position to Chris. The things he said sounded so sober, so staid, so member-of-the-community. This time Chris was serious.

"Eda, you're going too far. Serling doesn't answer your letters. Don't you see that?"

"No, and I don't care."

"Mary Wells doesn't answer your letters about going into the advertising business."

"She's too busy. I'll go down to New York and sit on her doorstep until she gives me a job. That's what a guy in the Auchinchloss novel did, and it worked."

"Eda, that was a novel. People don't do that in real life."

"Never mind. I received a letter of acknowledgment from Cronkite today."

"A three-cent postcard. They send one to everybody."

"Okay. Belittle the acknowledgment. You said that I would never get one."

That night when I watched television, the character looked at me directly. He was talking to me. Wherever I went, his eyes followed me. Chris looked different too. His narrow face, thin from being underweight, took on a sharper look. His eyebrows, which are thick and slanted upward, became thin. His lips drew a narrow line, and two short bumps started growing out of his forehead. His ears became longer and pointed, and his red hair turned to fire. I offered him a cup of coffee and went into the kitchen to set up the perk, telling myself that a change of scene would bring everything back into focus. It didn't work. The lid fell off the coffee can spilling the thousands of tiny brown granules on the kitchen floor. I cursed under my breath and got down on my knees hurriedly trying to scoop up the grains that danced in defiance before my sweaty hands.

"Having trouble?" boomed a voice that seemed to echo with hysterical laughter.

"No, nothing, I'll be in in a minute."

"Let me help you."

I looked up and twinged with pain. He had grown to the full height of the doorway. I looked down. The coffee in my hands had turned into worms.

"No, I don't need any help. Just be kind to me, whoever you are!"

I ran to the sink and quickly scrubbed off my hands.

"Eda, Eda, are you all right?"

I turned around and Satan had gone. Slowly, Chris's lips became fuller and there was a glow about his entire being. He was my angel husband.

That night, at bedtime, I asked Chris how people fell asleep.

"Eda, some people just relax and drift off into a world of their own. I can't really explain the process."

"Does it ever happen to them while they're awake? How do you know so many things?"

"Eda, at times you act like the most naïve child, whom I love and want to take care of, and at other times you're a viper—an uncontrollable bitch. You're basically a very mild person, but at times, I don't know what the hell gets into you. You change so rapidly that it's hard to keep track."

I knew what was happening. I was Eda, the way I wanted to be, the way I thought I should be, or I was dead. Whenever I was off my usual dosage of pills, I was afraid of being tired and afraid of being myself. My ambitions had to be fulfilled. I would drive down to New York and see Mary Wells. I'd sit on her doorstep until she gave me a job. If not Mary Wells, then I would go to Washington and put my cause to the people. Chris was scheduled to go to sea for a few days and I would have the car to myself.

The next day I drove Chris to the ship and kissed him good-bye. I promised a big surprise when he came back and then went home to make plans. I had the money. I jumped in the car and was on my way to New York.

About noontime, I began to feel the effect of a continual overdose of pep pills. The road became a blur and I had no idea of where I was really going. So I stopped at a small motel, got a room, and melted into the bedsheets without bothering to undress. When I woke up, it was the next day. Chris was due home in twelve hours. The trip to New York would be longer than I had expected and besides I was sober—dead sober. I wanted to turn to friends. I wanted advice. I popped two pills to boost my spirits and returned home. It wasn't time to own up.

When Chris came home, I was ecstatic and sexually hot. My vagina burned, tingled, and quivered. I was also under the illusion that I was on television. I would show the hidden cameras how beautiful a sex act could be.

I took Chris into the bedroom that was ablaze with the afternoon sun. The television cameras were well disguised. I took my time undressing and turned on the record player. Chris liked that. I draped my blouse around my breasts and arched forward. I shimmied to the swift beat of the rock music and let my long hair dance around my shoulders. I let him bite my tits and whispered, "Harder, Chris, harder. Kiss the belly," I implored. "Kiss the Duchess, man." When he entered my vagina with his tongue, it was fathomless. I would complete the total cycle: birth, death, and resurrection in this one act. I would give him a child in a matter of two days. Nine months was a lot of baloney. It was what you believed that counted. When I was satisfied, I whispered to a totally confused mate:

"The cycle has been completed."

"What cycle?"

"Birth, life, and death, all in one act. John Donne talked about it in his poetry. He said that to unite in the sexual union was to die for a short time."

"Eda, who's John Donne? What are you talking about?"

"John Donne preceded the metaphysical imagery of T. S. Eliot, and few people in his day appreciated his poetry or sermons. He lived and died as he saw fit."

"Eda, don't talk nonsense."

"I'm not. I have news for you. Tomorrow I'm having a very important visitor."

"Who?"

"I can't say. You might be disappointed if he doesn't come."

The President was coming. I expected congratulations on my recent efforts to negotiate with Chairman Mao. The expectation is hard to explain to anyone who knows reality. But life now was no longer real; it was delicious. All of the daydreams that one uses to escape or fulfill unsatisfied wants were the wings of my emotion. The President and his wife were stopping at my humble home. I had made the big league and was sure to be recognized for my achievements. A silent visit was all that I wanted. If they couldn't come, I was still happy. Sevareid and Cronkite answered my letters each night by their commentaries on television.

In my own world I was happy. But when I clashed with the realists—my husband, my parents, and my bar review cohorts—I realized that I no longer belonged. Chris was becoming aggravated. First, it was my failure to take the bar exam. Second, all the embarrassing letters to the newscasters. Third, my unexpected hallucinations. My illusion with the sun convinced him that something was wrong. I now had my own communication with God himself. When I wanted to watch television in the afternoon, the sun automatically lowered itself in the sky. No requests. It was merely a matter of desire.

One Sunday afternoon we went out for a ride, and Chris caught me staring at the blazing ball on the horizon.

"Eda, don't look at the sun. You'll blind yourself by looking at it directly."

"I'm looking at it right now and nothing's happening."

"What do you see in the sun anyway?"

"I see God. He exists in the sun just as He exists in the lit end of my cigarette. I am the Truth and the Light. That's what God said."

Our conversation stopped there. Chris turned his head to the side, but I saw the tears glistening in his eyes. He knew that somehow, some way, I was no longer with him.

On Monday, I went down to the drugstore as usual and ordered another batch of pills. As I was driving home, the sun beat down and Chris's tearstained face flashed before me. I heard his voice in the hollow gratings of the bridge plates as I drove over the river: "Eda, you're hurting me. I care about you and want you with me always." I pulled over to the side of the road and popped my last pill. Chris was too good to put up with my kind of game.

He trusted me without question, and I never met that trust. That night I owned up.

"Chris, I have a long story, and I don't know how to begin. I'm asking you to help me a second time."

"Will it explain your present behavior? Never mind. Go ahead."

"I've been on pep pills again."

"Have you taken any today?"

"Yes, I just got a refill."

"How long this time?"

"Since my sophomore year at law school."

"While you were still seeing the psychiatrist?"

"Yes."

"How many a day?"

"About thirty or forty. I haven't counted."

"Eda, you'll kill yourself if you don't quit. Why now?"

"I don't know. Maybe because I love you more than I loved my family. You might not understand, but you won't just bawl me out. I wanted to finish law school; I wanted to be a success. I wanted to be happy."

"Give me the pills. Give me all the prescriptions, and for God's sakes show me this time where you hid all this stuff."

For the next hour I opened up all the ripped linings of my purses, the hemlines of my dresses, the inside of my brassiere, and the undersides of cushions. The pills flowed —all kinds of pills—Preludin, Dexedrine, Methedrine, Deprol, Elavil, Tofranil, Soma, phenobarbital, and codeine.

"So this explains all the letters to Cronkite and Sevareid, the talk about going into advertising, the late-late midnight movies, the changes in the house?"

"No. I might have done all that on my own. I don't know. I won't ever know. Now that I've been on pep pills for about six years, I want a permanent out. But I'm afraid. You're going away tomorrow, and I don't know what's coming."

"You'll sleep. Try to sleep until I get home. But this time you're on your own. No doctors; no hospitals."

"Chris, you don't understand. I switch. Remember the

child and the viper in me. I don't know when I'm going to be one or the other. I can't control it anymore. I have another half, and I don't know who's going to win out."

"Eda, I'll take care of you."

"You don't know what you're asking for, man. You just have no idea."

That night I slept without the aid of pills. I took Chris to the boat the next morning and went back to bed for two whole days. When I finally woke up, I dragged myself into the kitchen, gobbled down some moldy cheese and stale bread, and poured back into bed. Sleep exhausted me. I knew that I would feel that way until I was entirely slept out.

Chris hadn't arrived home yet. I had one more day to wait. For the first time in six years I had no compulsion to do anything. I forced myself to go through the motions of cleaning up the house, but I didn't have the old energy or the interest that pep pills gave me. I wanted my pills—some of my God food—to lift me up, thin as air and made of gossamer wings.

I searched through my purses, under the bed, and found one pill that I had missed in my confession to Chris. I gobbled it down with glee and felt tense about my plight. I searched again—much harder—and came up with a second pill. I was awake, but I didn't have the interest. I only had the energy and those two pills were all I had.

In a panic, I called Grace, the commanding officer's wife: "Grace, Eda. Chris's out on the ship. Grace, I've been on pep pills—lots of them. I need a doctor. I can't do it on my own like Chris wanted me to. I've been taking 1,000 milligrams of amphetamines a day, and I'm coming down. Help me."

"Hold the fort, we'll be over to pick you up. I know, Eda. I've had a nervous breakdown myself."

When Grace and her husband arrived, they looked at me not knowing what to expect and fearing the worst.

"Did you pack a nightgown, Eda?"

"No. I just wanted some advice."

"They may want you to stay overnight."

"I can't do that. Chris's coming home tomorrow. I've got to be home to greet him. They can give me something to take at home."

"Okay, but they may want you back in the morning."

We arrived at the base hospital near midnight. The doctor in charge prescribed some tranquilizers and suggested that I come back to see the base psychiatrist as soon as possible.

The next day, I told Chris about the appointment that I needed with the psychiatrist.

"You can't get over it at home?"

"No."

"You promised this time you'd get over it without hospitals, doctors, or tranquilizers. Why didn't you keep that promise, Eda?"

"Because I need a doctor."

"A doctor won't help you. You have to help yourself."

"I can help myself to a certain extent, but I'm sick."

"You're not sick. Don't go to some nutty psychiatrist. I'll stay home and help you."

"Make an appointment and let me take the tranquilizers."

"Okay. I'll make the appointment. But nothing's wrong with you. You've just got a complex about taking pills. Make up your mind that you alone have the strength to overcome anything that you want."

"Chris, I want to see a doctor—tomorrow."

"Eda, as soon as you find someone like your father who tells you what to do, life's a lot easier. I want you to think for yourself. You're twenty-five years old. You're a lawyer. You speak four languages. You have to grow up and face life."

"You don't know what's going to happen to me. The last time I went off drugs, I was wild. You never saw me at the hospital until I was halfway sane. I don't want to go through it again. This time I want to come out of it and be the way I was six years ago, although I can't remember back that far. If I have your help and the doctor's help, maybe I can make it."

"Eda, I love you. Doctors are only interested in your money."

"Make the appointment, Chris—please."

"Are you still taking the tranquilizers?"

"Yes. They keep me from believing and seeing things the way I saw them before."

The next day, I waited with Chris outside the office of Dr. Judd Liebowitz, the base psychiatrist. He wanted to see me alone. He looked like a kindly man who was interested in the tortured, twisted histories of most of his patients. We sat down. He adjusted his glasses and asked me one simple question that I was unable to answer.

"Why, Eda Spaight?"

"Why? Because my father wants me to be a lawyer; my family wants me to be a success. Chris wants me to stay off drugs and tells me that all you are after is his money. My sister Angelina tells me to forget the whole goddamn business about being a lawyer, forget about Papa, and teach languages."

"Eda Spaight, what do you want to do?"

"I don't know. If I knew in the first place, I would have stayed off pills and told everyone else to go to hell like I did six years ago. When I went to college with straight A's out of high school, all my relatives told me that I would either flunk out or find a nice man, get married, and raise a family like everyone else. I heard the same goddamn shit when I started law school. Chris showed me that married life didn't have to mean stagnation. He's the only one I've really failed. I've breached a trust. I don't know if I did the right thing in coming here because Chris thinks that all doctors don't care about me as much as he does and he's probably right. Do you think that you can help?"

"I'll see, Mrs. Spaight. But I would like to speak to your husband and then to you again."

I waited outside. When Chris came out of the office he looked at me gravely. It was my turn to hear the decision. Dr. Liebowitz put it to me bluntly:

"Mrs. Spaight, I'll try something new with you and hope that it works. I don't want to admit you to the state mental hospital. The ball rests with you. We have no ward for psychiatric care on the base. But I'll admit you to the regular hospital as one of my special cases. You need lots of rest and time to discover yourself. I'll visit you every day and keep you on a fairly heavy dosage of tranquilizers. You should be all right in two or three weeks. But since you've been on pills before, I can't trust you until you prove yourself."

"What about Chris? He promised to take care of me. I don't want to leave him."

"Chris has agreed. He'll stop over and visit you. Come, we'll see about getting you into the hospital."

The base hospital was across the street. It accommodated all patients—from cancer to maternity. I was promptly given some pills, put in a hospital gown, and politely ordered to bed. I went to sleep but woke up in the middle of the night. I wasn't sleepy so I wandered out to talk to the night nurse. She had other orders.

"Mrs. Spaight, come in here, please." She ushered me into an empty room.

"Dr. Liebowitz ordered an extra dosage of Thorazine if you can't sleep. Please roll over. It won't hurt for more than a minute."

"Dr. Liebowitz didn't tell me anything about a needle. I'm a human being."

"Mrs. Spaight, please roll over or I'll have to call for help."

"Don't. I'm not violent. I just don't understand and I'm trying my best to behave. I like to be treated like an adult. Ouch! Can I sit and talk until the medicine takes effect?"

"No. Doctor's orders are to go back to bed."

I dragged myself back into bed and soon passed out. When I woke up, there was another nurse and another order to take tranquilizers.

"The doctor wants you to eat breakfast."

"You can tell the doctor that on this dosage I'm only capable of hibernation. Bears don't even have it this good. Good night."

I slept until the attendant came with lunch. I picked at the carrots, dropped the fork on the floor, and rolled over.

The nurse came in the afternoon with more pills. I got up to go to the bathroom, fell asleep, and had to be escorted back to bed. The nurses urged me to get up, but it was like offering a crutch to a corpse. Chris came to see me, but I was incoherent. He quietly brushed the hair away from my forehead, gave me a kiss, and left. Liebowitz walked in later on.

"How are you feeling?"

"Droopy. If you weren't right here, I wouldn't know I had a visitor. I'm going to pass out."

"You haven't moved from your bed for three days."

"I don't want to. I can't even stay awake in the john."

"Maybe it's time to decrease your dosage."

"Not if I get shots at night. You didn't tell me about the shots and I trusted you."

"No more shots, Eda."

"If you want to help me, you have to realize that all nuts aren't violent."

The lower dosage was ineffective. I slept. It helped to pass the time in between visits.

Dr. Liebs (as I now called him) was kind to me. But every time that I got up, I felt dizzy. When I started to walk, my legs collapsed and I felt sick to my stomach. I didn't feel right walking around in a hospital gown. There were too many men for me to feel comfortable with an open caboose. Liebs accommodated me and told Chris to bring a bathrobe. I was pleased but unenthusiastic.

When Liebs decreased the dosage again, I got up. There was little to do but sit and watch television. I'd only talk for a few hours, pass into a semi-stupor, and be ushered back into bed.

A week went by without incident. Dr. Liebs kept decreasing my dosage. I started to help deliver meals, make the beds, and do the general clean-up work. Few people believed that I was a mental case.

In the meantime, I had many talks with Dr. Liebs. I told him that I liked to embroider but had difficulty concentrating on the difficult stitches. I'd get interested in one thing and then I'd get restless. He suggested that I be allowed to go outside and walk around the hospital building.

In our sessions, I told Dr. Liebs about my former ambitions to be a great lawyer. I didn't have the slightest idea of what I was like six years before I started on pep pills. I thought that I was fat. I was an honors student and participated in every activity imaginable. When I started on drugs, everything was thrown aside for the higher goal of becoming a lawyer. I had talked law, thought law, and lived law for four years.

"But did you really like law?" Dr. Liebs asked.

"I'm not sure. I drummed the idea into my head so hard that I never thought about it."

One day after a fight with Chris, I switched from the rational Eda to my old self. I'd already been classified as a schizophrenic. When Chris came in, we took a seat away from the other patients.

"How are you doing, Eda?"

"Dr. Liebs says I'll be out of here in two weeks provided nothing goes wrong."

"What does that mean?"

"I settle down and decide on a logical plan of action, like staying home and doing something constructive."

"Sounds good for a change."

"He's stifling my ambitions. He's already said that I'm not sick. Why is he keeping me here? I don't belong. This is a place for sick people."

"Eda, give him time."

"Hell, I'm dying here, Chris. He doesn't discuss his problems with me. It's all a one-way street. And you're no better. You're all for mediocrity and conformity. I'll act well enough to get out of here and then I'll start my own reform and make all you guys look sick—psychiatrists included. I'll go to see Mary Wells in New York and join her ad agency, or I'll set up my own reform in Washington. I won't be well but at least I'll be different. Dr. Liebs feels that as long as I conform, as long as I do things the way my parents did them and everybody else does them, I'm okay. I'll play the game. That's all it is—a silly little game. I thought you were made of stronger stuff, Chris, but I see now that you're no different than all the others."

"Eda, I'd better leave. I upset you, and you aren't making sense. I'll come back tomorrow when you feel better."

"You said that there was nothing wrong with me. Chris, I believed what you said."

"Eda, you change so rapidly. I can't tell whether you make any sense."

"I don't. Every time I start talking about things that I really believe in, I'm told that I'm sick. It's not easy to forget my own identity and start thinking like everyone else. I have to change my whole personality. It hurts. I feel like I'm dying and I'm not sure that a person that I'll like is going to be reborn. I'm talking figuratively, but it's the only way that I can think right now."

After my talk with Chris, Liebs upped my dosage of Thorazine, and I slowly reverted to a more peaceful person. But since I still had a split personality, I felt that I betrayed myself by returning to the world of the living. I had been in my own world so long that the step down, the similarity to sane people, was stifling. I couldn't believe that Chris really wanted me that way.

My first week at the hospital had passed. I was now well established as helper at the nurses' desk, working long hours on charts. The charts were boring and monotonous, but at least I could see my accomplishment. I had to stay busy. It gave me a sense of well-being. Best of all, I was trusted.

The nurses remarked on my progress to Dr. Liebs, and we had frequent talks. I was still going through the big "ups and downs." One day I would feel that I had clear insight and a purpose to what I did. On other days, my former beliefs would haunt me.

I hadn't told anyone about my hallucinations with the television set—that all programs were in direct response to the content of my former letters. When I finally told Dr. Liebs, he asked: "But you realize that Chris was right? You realize that the letters were probably discarded as crank mail?"

"No. The connection is too direct. I've talked to you about the Powell incident. When the Supreme Court of New York mentioned the game of 'cops and robbers,' how could I help but believe that I had had some influence? It was in the book that I sent them. You see, in my former world, everything was related to everything else. It all made sense to me."

"Eda, you have to watch out. Sometimes you don't make sense to me or the nurses. The more you forget your former ideas, the better you will be. At times you skip from one subject to the next so fast that no one can tell what you're thinking. It's characteristic of your condition."

"Am I having another nervous breakdown?"

"That covers a lot of evils. I wish people, including doctors, wouldn't use the term. It includes a thousand individual cases that can't be explained. How do you feel here?"

"I've managed to concentrate more on my embroidery and I help serve the meals. But I'm not calm enough to sit down and watch the tube."

"You think that's dangerous anyway. Why don't you start to read?"

"Reading is the same as watching the tube. Everything I read I misinterpret. I see the main character of every novel as myself. I throw myself into the plot so deeply and identify so much with the character that I want to write the author and tell him, 'Thank you for expressing my feelings.' When I hear music that I like, every vein in my body pumps double-time—I play it over and over and dance to it. Drives everyone else in the place crazy. I live the music, my head bobs to the rock beat, I hum the music, my vocal chords strum the music, I sing . . ."

"That's enough. You're rambling again. I'll increase your dosage so that you can relax. In the meantime, try to read."

By the third week in the hospital, I graduated to wearing most of my ordinary clothes around the ward. I socialized with some of the orderlies who came to visit us. Dr. Liebs kept me under a stiff dosage of Thorazine all along.

My stay was prolonged another week. I was beginning to dip into the "lows" and experience odd surges of emotion that were unpredictable. Nevertheless, Liebs authorized a trial visit home.

As I waited for Chris on the back porch of the hospital, I began reciting the "Lord's Prayer." I hummed the words to myself as I heard it sung at my wedding when Papa, with tears in his eyes, had said: "Mother and I give away Eda, our last daughter." I began to heave big sobs and then to cry. Chris came along.

"Eda, what's the matter?"

"Oh, Chris. I was humming the 'Lord's Prayer.' Do you think that God will ever forgive me? Will Papa and Mama forgive me a second time? Will you forgive me for making such a mess out of a young life? I've sinned twice. I heard the words of the 'Lord's Prayer' echoing into the sunset. This world is so beautiful. I want to stay in it."

"Let's go, Tiger."

It was my first weekend home. Chris had cleaned the house from top to bottom. He had thrown out the newspaper clippings and all my writing materials. He had washed the windows, removed the kites, and rearranged the furniture. My homemade world of fantasy had been soaked, stripped, and replaced with a spanking clean apartment. I was as bitter as Aladdin who had lost his magic lamp, but we were going to start anew.

I took my medicine faithfully, so things went smoothly. That evening we discussed my future plans. Liebs had suggested applying for a job that didn't tax my brain at the outset.

We ate at home that night, and, knowing no other method when it came to the dishes, I pulled out my plastic bucket, set it on the drainboard, and soaked the dishes in Mr. Clean. Chris came in with the idea of getting me to abandon this practice once and for all.

"But, Chris, this way, I save all the mess and fuss of taking out the drainboard and then putting it away."

"Eda, there are a lot of old habits that I'm going to have to change."

"Why? There you go again. The way your mother did things. I've already lost the magic of my existence. If you're going to show me reality, you're going to have to teach me to like it."

"But, Eda, the kitchen is a constant mess. My way only takes a minute. Just try it for once."

"I'm not convinced. Maybe I never did things right, but I did them my way."

"Did you take your pill today?"

"Yes, but it's not going to change my mind."

Chris had one hell of a time convincing me that it was useless to polish my good-luck ring any more, and we still disagreed over the interpretation of my effect on the television. Yet, all in all, I merited a good report on my return to the hospital that Sunday. I had one more trial visit, one more week in the hospital, and then I was home free.

It was drawing close to departure time. On the last visit, Dr. Liebs advised me to be faithful to the Thorazine.

When the day finally arrived, I was excited and perplexed. I had nothing planned, and Liebs felt that a structured existence was very important. He advised Chris to stay with me over the weekend and to arrive home as early as possible.

Our first days at home were uneventful. Chris tried to do everything. I tried cleaning. But now when I cleaned a room, it was a matter of minutes. Reading books was out. It meant sitting. Sitting meant not exercising, and not exercising meant gaining weight. I soon ran out of things to do. I didn't want to bake because it meant eating. I was off pep pills and afraid. If I started to cook like Aunt Gabriella, I might eat and end up looking just like her. The whole program of years before loomed before my eyes.

I took my dosage in the morning and went back to bed. It was a nice escape. Chris encouraged me to stay up and find new interests. "I can't." That was my basic attitude. I can't because I don't know. Liebs had warned me that adjusting to the outside would be difficult. I couldn't explain my feeling of despair and lack of direction to Chris.

He suggested that I decrease my dosage. I cut down but failed to realize the cumulative effect of tranquilizers for keeping me on an even keel. I soon felt my old self returning. I perked up. I formed opinions, and then one night I returned to the base hospital.

As I was talking to Chris, I turned on the television. It was late and the show was a thriller. Chris told me to turn it off and go to bed. It was too late. The show was telling me something. Chills started going up and down my spine. The old frozen dreams that I had experienced in the past were returning—only this time I was awake. I glanced at Chris. He wasn't the gentle Chris that I loved and wanted to please. He had changed into the monstrous demon of a few weeks before. I sensed immediate danger and had to get out of the apartment. I said something noncommittal and eased toward the door. In a fast move, I yanked the handle and tried to open it. Chris grabbed my arm.

"Eda, what did I say? Eda, are you all right?"

"Goddamnit, let go of me, Satan! I'm going where people will listen to me. I'm going down to Washington. You're all trying to change me and I don't want to be changed. I've brought this on myself and now I'm leaving."

"Eda, listen to me. Eda, come back."

I made my way out of the door and was halfway down the hall when Chris came and dragged me back into the apartment.

"Eda, let's talk this over."

"All right, but I'm going to Washington and get away from all this shit."

Once again we sat down to watch television. The same horror story was on. It concerned the mental ward of a state hospital. Since I had been on a mental ward once before, I wasn't frightened. I understood the people. Slowly, the lights around me began to dim. The light from my favorite lamp cast a rainbow against the wall, which magnified Chris's shadow and tinged his features with reflections of orange and red—the colors of hell. Again he was Satan. My life was now in danger. He was no longer my husband. I had to leave.

I never made it past the emergency lock. Chris had bolted the door, so there was no escape. The telephone was too far away. I was in a room with the devil himself.

"Eda, I'll take you to the hospital."

"You're not taking me anywhere because you're not my husband, you're Satan. My husband is Chris Spaight. What did you do to him? Who are you?"

"Eda, you'd better take a pill."

"Yes, take a pill. But you told me not to take pills. It's too late anyway."

"Take a pill and we'll go to the hospital."

"I don't want to. I want to stay here."

"You're not ready to stay home. Let's go see the doctor."

We arrived at the hospital, and I was immediately ushered into the ward. The nurses welcomed me back as a visitor. I sat down and asked for a cup of coffee and started to sip it. I explained that Chris was there to see the doctor. One of the nurses was getting married and was sewing her wedding dress.

"I have a secret."

"Want to tell us about it?"

"Have you ever heard of a virgin birth?"

"Yes."

"I can't be sure but in six hours I'm going to have a baby. I didn't want to wait nine months like all the rest of the women in the maternity ward. They're all so inactive, misshapen, and lonely for their husbands who are out on boats. Nine months is a lot of baloney."

"That's very interesting."

"That's why Chris brought me here. He wants me to deliver in the hospital."

"Really?"

As I continued to talk, my voice got loud. I stopped talking about my impending delivery and switched to other subjects. I sat near the window and was soon the only one talking—only now I was shouting.

"It's too bad all the goddamn men in the world don't treat their wives better. Goddamnit, if they want to go shopping, they should have free rein. Husbands and wives break up because the goddamn men don't appreciate all that their women do for them. They stay away the whole goddamn day and expect the housework done, the children fed, the meal ready, and a happy wife on top of that. If they throw the goddamn newspaper on the floor, they want it picked up. The sons of bitches act like God."

"Mrs. Spaight, will you come into the other room?"

I was hoarse from shouting. Most of the patients were awake and came in to see what was going on. I followed the nurse into the room for the same deflating routine that I had undergone the first night.

"Roll over, please, I have to give you a needle. It won't hurt but a minute."

"I don't need a needle. There's nothing wrong with me."

"Please, I have my instructions and I don't want to call for help."

When the needle penetrated, I believed that the tip had broken off and remained in my buttocks. I said nothing but felt the pain of the imagined needle for days.

In fifteen minutes, I was in a stupor. Chris dragged me home under strict instructions to bring me back to the doctor's office the next day. I was to be committed to the state mental hospital. I would find out that hell doesn't exist in some after-world down below. It exists on earth—in a state mental hospital.

The next day, Chris packed my bags and told me that we were going to the doctor's office. When I entered, Dr. Liebowitz told me to sit down as he had something important to say. I was docile and groggy.

"Eda, I've made arrangements for you to go to the hospital. Your case is more serious than I had anticipated."

"Where?"

"It's not very far away and Chris will visit you from time to time."

"But I don't want to leave home. I don't want to leave Chris."

"It's necessary at this time."

"Is it a nice place?"

"Not exactly, but they'll be able to deal with you there."

"You said that I was finished with the hospital—that I was on the road to recovery."

"Eda, you need treatment that I can't give you here."

"I don't want to go. Chris thinks that I'm okay. I don't want any more needles or any more pills. Every time I open my mouth and talk about what I really think, you say that I belong in the hospital."

"Eda, I, too, will come to see you."

I left the office not knowing what to think. I didn't know what to expect from hospital, doctor, or husband. On the road to the hospital, I was docile. I was still under the impression that I was pregnant and we were going in for delivery. Chris was very quiet. My visions of him as Satan had stopped, so I was safe.

The lobby of the state hospital was modern, pleasant, and bare of any decoration. We waited at the admissions desk for a half hour. Chris went to find someone, and we waited another hour. He was irritable while I was complacent. I was only going to be there a few days. After I had the baby, I would go home. It fitted the cycle that I had experienced that night at home under the lights of the television cameras: birth, life, and death repeated. This was the creative part of our lives. We were the new Mary and Joseph—the modern version of the Bible relived in the present. How lucky I was to be the chosen woman. I would bring the world back to sanity again. I would bear the genius who would show the rest of society how to live.

Finally an admitting clerk ushered us into a small room. She took my name, which I could no longer spell, my address which Chris gave her, his occupation, and the routine information about the family. She made a few phone calls for an escort and waited. A nurse came down from one of the many floors of the maze. Chris took my bags and handed them to me.

"Can't my husband come with me to see my room?"

"No, he can't. He'll come to visit you during the visiting hours."

"But Chris always helps me to unpack, especially in my condition."

"Mrs. Adams will keep you company. Your husband will have to leave."

"But I've never left my husband. You don't understand. I love my husband and I'm going to have a baby."

"Mrs. Spaight, it's almost time for lunch."

"Chris, will you come to see me?"

"Yes, my dearest Eda."

"When?"

"As soon as I can."

"Chris, I don't know what I'm doing in this place. I'm a human being. I'm afraid."

"Eda, I'll come to see you very soon."

"Mrs. Spaight, will you please go with Mrs. Adams."

Chris tugged my hand and gave me the tenderest kiss a man could ever give a sick woman. He told me later that he went home and cried that night. I was too incoherent at the time to understand the heartbreak when a member of one's family is committed to a mental institution.

I accompanied Mrs. Adams down the long corridors. They were made of gray cement block, and there were thick bars on the windows. Mrs. Adams took me up a padded elevator to my designated floor. At the entrance to the elevator was another escort. I was ushered into a separate room and asked to undress. The procedure was painless. I suffered no shame and talked calmly to Mrs. Adams and the escort. Outside I saw the lights of the television cameras. I heard the crowds clapping. I had done it. I had conquered the inhibitions of the American woman and was now showing her that it was no sin to be televised in the nude. Why should she be ashamed of her body?

I kept all these thoughts to myself. Had I mentioned the cameras, I would have been placed in solitary. After the exam, it was lunchtime. I wasn't hungry, so I spent a few minutes in the lounge getting acquainted.

I walked over to one woman and introduced myself. No answer. I saw another woman seated over in the corner with both hands tied to a chair. I introduced myself and received a cold, angry stare. A third woman said: "Don't talk to her. She's dangerous."

With nothing else to do, I asked one of the nurses where to get lunch. She ushered me down a long gray corridor. There was a line and a few patients who were friendly and talkative.

"How are the meals here?"

"Lousy. You're lucky if you can get something edible."

"That doesn't make any difference. I'm not very hungry."

"You'd better eat. They're very concerned around here that you eat well."

"My name is Eda Spaight. I'm glad to meet you."

"My name is Lou Sanders. I work here. Here the workers eat with the patients. Are you new here?"

"Yes. I just came today."

"You'll get used to the place. There's not much to do but eat and sleep."

"I keep hearing them page a Dr. Wing. Is he the head of the hospital?"

"They page doctors all the time. There's such a shortage of them."

By this time I had reached the end of the food line. I took a salad and some custard.

"My, but you aren't very hungry."

"Well, some of it looked good, but I'm very tired."

"Join us for lunch? You don't act like most of the people around here."

I picked at my lunch. The food was bland, and I was more interested in having people to talk to.

Lou asked: "Have you met any of the other patients?"

"Yes, but they don't talk to me."

"They get that way after being here a while. Why don't you try and talk to some of the other patients?"

I saw a young girl sitting at the table all by herself. She had put on entirely too much makeup. She had smeared lipstick over half her face. The eye shadow on her lids extended almost up to her brows and the mascara ran down the lower part of her eyelids forming two black lines around the rim of her eyes. It was a sad sight. I excused myself from the group that I was with and joined this hideous-looking girl for the last half of my lunch. I introduced myself and asked to join her.

"Why?"

"I thought that you might like some company."

"Nobody talks to me. I'm a bitch. But I don't care. I don't like them either." She pointed to another group seated across from us. The women at this table were older, wore no makeup, and one of them had long curly black hair. Her name was Betty.

"Betty hates me."

"Why?" I asked.

"Because I'm pregnant and I have a boy friend. My name is Rita."

"Oh?"

"Eat your custard. You must eat your custard."

"But I'm full."

"Never mind. Eat your custard. It's the only thing around here. Do I look nice? Betty says I'm a whore."

"I don't know. Excuse me. I think I'll go to my room. I'm very tired."

At this point I found one of the nurses and told her that I wanted to lie down. I was ushered into a room with six empty beds. When I woke up, a doctor was by my bedside. He had black curly hair and a moustache.

"Doctor, where am I?"

"You're here for a rest."

"Are you Spanish? *Entonces puedo explicarlo todo en español.* I must explain the whole story in Spanish because only one who comes from a Latin background can understand it."

I continued in Spanish: "My father is the greatest person in the world. I wanted to be a lawyer—to be the greatest professional in the East. My father was a wonderful man. But he was Latin. He was strong. I'm strong like that too, Doctor, and when I get out of here, I want to continue my profession. I took pep pills so that I could study harder. I wanted to achieve. Now I'm here and I don't know why. I tried to do so much to change the system. When can I leave? When can I go home to see my husband who loves me? I want to see Dr. Wing who they keep paging all the time."

"Señora, I'm impressed with your intelligence and knowledge of my language. Most of the people here aren't as intelligent as you are. You will find it difficult here, but you need a rest. I will come to you from time to time, or another doctor will come to see you. Hopefully, you won't have to stay too long."

"But, Doctor, I have no friends here. I have no one."

"Mrs. Spaight, you must relax here."

"Who's this I see? Judy from school. Judy, what are you doing here?"

The nurse who had approached was puzzled by my familiarity. The doctor sensed that I was still hallucinating and must have suggested that she play along. I heard him whisper to the nurse, "Her name is Eda," but I was unable to grasp its significance.

I continued, "Judy, I knew that you were in nursing school, but I never expected to see you here in Connecticut. Do you still play the clarinet? I gave up on the violin when I entered law school."

"Eda, I've come to help you. Anything that you want, don't hesitate to ask me."

"Judy, you're the first soul I've seen in this place. Can I trust you? Do you give needles? I'm very sleepy, Doctor. Can I go to sleep?"

"Of course, Eda. I'll try to get in touch with your father."

"Doctor, I want to see my Chris. When can I see my husband?"

When I awoke, it was dark. It must have been around ten at night. I got up quietly, thinking that there must be a way out of the place. I wanted to go home. From the moment that I had arrived, all I could think of was leaving. I met one of the patients in the hallway. She had gray eyes and her face looked blue in the dark hallway light. Her name was Claire, and she told me that in private life she'd been a nurse, but had taken an overdose of amphetamines. I talked with her until one of the night nurses came along.

"Mrs. Spaight. It's time for you to take your pill. You were sleeping when I gave the pills out."

"All right. But first I've got to go to the bathroom."

"It's right down the hall."

"I'll be right back."

The bathroom was the same place where I had undressed for the preliminary exam. But then I hadn't looked at it closely. Now I was horrified and scared. There were no doors on the toilet stalls. I entered the first stall. There was either water or urine all over the floor. Wet toilet paper was strewn over the top of the toilet. The toilet wasn't flushed, and I gagged and went to the next stall. Same thing. I felt weak and nauseous, but I had to go. I hated the thought of walking through someone else's piss and going in a filthy toilet.

While I was in the bathroom, my fears were heightened by hysterical yelling that I heard in the background. I was almost too scared to move or leave. I hadn't seen many nurses on the night shift. Would there be enough to keep everyone in order? I wanted to take a shower but didn't dare without a guard. I left the bathroom and there was no nurse to be seen. I went into the lounge where a small group of patients were sitting and talking; one of them was Betty. She had mean eyes. I sat down quietly while Betty stared at me. I had the feeling that she could be violent. The members of the group asked me why I was there. I told my story and said that I was very lonesome for my husband.

"Don't hang around with Rita," Betty said. "She's no good."

"All right. I know that she's not like me. I was a virgin when I got married."

"Glad to hear it," Betty said. "You don't look like the type."

"I suppose I don't look like a lawyer either."

"A lawyer?"

"Yes."

"Well then, they really had to be nuts to lock you up in here."

I didn't tell the group what I was thinking at the time. God had put me in the state hospital. He had put me there for a reason and only for one night. I was a Christmas present to these people. Our whole nocturnal visit with each other was being nationally televised. I, sound, sane Eda, had volunteered to go into a state mental institution to talk to these patients. I would probably be released the next day. I was sincere and figured that the only way to get along with them was to understand and act just like them. If I were accepted as one of them, I wouldn't be the object of their more violent hates. I was also afraid for my own safety.

"Why are you really here, Eda?" Betty asked.

"For believing in people, for trusting in people, and for taking an overdose of pep pills. I'm coming down. Sometimes I get so uptight that I want to scream. I can't sleep."

"We know, dearie, we've all been through it."

"Right now though, I'm very tired. Where can I sleep?"

"I'll get one of the nurses. She'll show you where to sleep."

One of the nurses came and showed me a bed. It was the bed next to the dangerous woman I had met earlier and I couldn't fall asleep. My body became numb. As I lay there in a semi-coma, I could again hear the crowds outside applauding. Eda, you've done it. You have entered a mental institution—the most Godforsaken place on the face of the earth—to bring your goodwill to the many inmates. Tomorrow you will be rewarded for your boldness.

When the numbness wore off, I was up again, and I went directly to the lobby. Betty was no longer there. She had been carried off to her padded cell in a different ward. Claire and another patient were still seated. Now was the time to act my part. I began breathing heavily with the excuse that I couldn't sleep—that the pep pills were bothering me again. Claire suggested that I take it easy, just sit down with them and talk. She had been through the same thing before. She called it the "pep shakes." I felt that I was speaking her language. This was what God wanted—communication with these people. Suddenly a nurse showed up.

"My, are you people staying up late."

"Eda can't sleep."

"Oh, Mrs. Spaight. I forgot to give you your pill. Come with me."

"I think I need a pill. I need something."

"Take your pill and go to bed."

It was a long evening. I took my pill but couldn't sleep. It was only around one in the morning when I was awakened by a nurse with a needle in her hand. I rolled over subconsciously and took the needle. Claire was there and took my pulse. Her gray eyes and pale blue face faded into the distance. "Good God, she's fainted."

I heard all this in the soft distance, but I hadn't really fainted, just fallen asleep. I slept an hour and was up again. This time the nurse was emphatic about my going to bed and staying in bed.

"But I want to go home. I realize that I must only spend one night in this place. Please. I must go home."

"Mrs. Spaight, I think that you had better sleep in a separate room tonight."

The nurse took me by the hand and led me through some glass doors and down another corridor to a room. The walls were made of blue cement block, broken only by one small window. And overhead a bulb glared down upon a bed, the only furnishing. The thick heavy metal door to the room creaked as it opened. It had a lock and a peephole.

"There, Mrs. Spaight. You sleep in here tonight."

"But where are the other patients? I really don't like a room all to myself. There's no one to talk to."

"Just a minute, Mrs. Spaight. I'll be right back."

As soon as the nurse had gone, I felt it was time to escape. I hated the room and wanted to be with the other patients. Even though I was afraid of them, it was better than being alone. I pushed the door open before the nurse returned to lock me in. There was nothing at that end of the hall, so I tugged at another door that I thought might be the rear exit to the building. That didn't work and I was becoming desperate. The hell with the whole goddamn idea of representing God and helping these people. I didn't belong in this place. I was sane.

I found my way to another door at the end of another corridor. It was a glass door, but I could see that there were elevators behind it that led to the outside. I tried to open the door and it was locked. Through the door and beyond were the padded cells where they kept people like Betty when she had to go to sleep. There was only a chance that it was an escape route. Why, oh why, didn't Chris come to see me? Why didn't Mom come to get me out of this awful place?

The nurses found me on the floor, tugging at the glass door.

"I think we had better get the octopus," one of them said.

"What's the octopus?" I asked. "What are you going to do to me?"

"Come with us, Mrs. Spaight. Back to your new room. You should have been in bed hours ago."

"I told you that I'm scared. Please."

I went back to the cement cell, escorted on both sides. I got into bed and asked the nurse to turn off the light and lock the door.

One of the other nurses entered with a long piece of muslin.

"Don't put that thing on me. I haven't done anything wrong. I'm just scared of this place and all the hysterical yelling and all the rest of the patients. You don't know how scared I am."

Claire soon appeared beside my bed. Her face was blue again from the reflection of the walls and the dim light. She looked like a saint. She told me to be quiet.

"But, Claire, I'm not shouting. Don't you understand that it was all a joke. I'm sane. I was placed here and I guess I put on a good show of acting like the rest of you. I had to. Otherwise, Betty might have gotten after me."

In the meantime, I was squirming, trying to avoid the various loops that were being thrown around me. The octopus was a long piece of muslin that the nurses coiled around me. When they finished, my feet were spread apart, each one tied to the posts on the bed, and my arms were raised above my head and tied to the head of the bed. Whenever I tried to move my neck, the piece around it tightened. I was crucified to the bed. Such a medieval device assured the nurses that I couldn't move in any way for the rest of the night.

It must have been around three in the morning when I woke up. I had to go to the bathroom since my bowels were loose due to the medication. I was also nauseous from the shots that I had received earlier. The room was still dark. I called out for help. I tried to move, but the octopus pulled tighter around my neck. God, oh God, why do you do this to your people? Why do you expose them to such horror, such pain, and then say that human beings aren't capable of redeeming themselves? They don't give a shit in here whether or not you die from urinosis.

With that, I gave up the ghost and went in the bed. I urinated and moved my bowels. The urine stank and became sticky as it trickled down my legs. Again I called out for someone—anyone. I was lying in my own feces. The smell was making me nauseous and yet I couldn't move. I didn't want to vomit, but the smell of the urine and feces was working on my weak stomach. I held back and then it came. Since my hands were tied as well as my legs, the vomit splattered all over my chin and ran down into my hair. God, now I was really sick. I tried to call out again but choked on a piece of undigested salad.

In two hours everything had caked: the urine, the feces, and the vomit. No one came and that made my situation all the more pitiful. I called out again: Mama, Papa, Chris, help!

Two hours later, I heard the door unlock. The nurse stood there with a needle. Not another needle! What did

I do? She turned on the light above the bed and looked at me—pitiful, scared mess that I was.

"Mrs. Spaight, shame on you. What a mess you are!"

I must have looked inhuman: vomit in my hair and all over my face, shit in my pants and dried urine all over my legs. I began to sob.

"How could I help it? I called and called for someone to help me and untie me, and when no one came, I gave up. Doesn't anyone listen?"

"If you behave yourself tonight, maybe you can sleep in the other room."

"Tonight? I won't be here tonight. My husband's coming to take me out of here today."

"It's time to eat breakfast. Here, let me get you out of this. I guess you don't need another injection. Now why don't you go down the hall and have a good breakfast?"

"I'm sorry, but sleeping in my feces and having vomit slop around my neck kind of ruins the appetite."

"Then why don't you change your clothes and go out in the lobby?"

"I'd like to, but no one out there talks to me."

"I think that you're scheduled for a talk with the doctor. He makes his rounds this morning."

"Good. I want to see that Dr. Wing that they've been paging all night."

"Mrs. Spaight, they don't page anyone in your ward."

"That's all I could hear all last night. He's the head of the hospital, isn't he?"

"I've never heard of the doctor that you're talking about."

Anxious for company, I moved out into the lobby. It was a pathetic sight. Everyone was sitting around with nothing to do and nothing to say to each other. Rita, the unwed mother, was there with her usual pile of makeup. Suddenly she stood up, lifted up her dress, and pulled down her pants, exposing her vagina.

"So I'm bad, so I was loose, so I loved him. What does it matter to the rest of you?"

Betty entered the room and looked at me with a cold

stare. I was stunned but said nothing, just walked over to Betty.

"I heard you had a rough time last night, kid," she said. "I used to be a nurse so I know what it's like. I told you not to talk to Rita. Just look at that little bitch. You can talk to me though. I'm on good behavior here. They let me hand out pills and do things to help the nurses."

"But, Betty, I'm supposed to go home today."

"That's what they all say, kid, until the place drives you crazy. People who come here stay here."

"Betty, who's Dr. Wing? I hear them calling his name all the time."

"I don't know, Eda. Just a personal problem of yours. Better get some breakfast."

"I'm not hungry."

"That's all there is to do around here, eat, sleep, and die. If you're lucky, your doctor will come to see you once in a while."

"I think I'll try to get to know some of the other patients."

"Don't."

"Why?"

"Because they just aren't the type of people you'll get along with. Claire is okay because she's leaving soon. I'm okay. But watch out for the rest."

Rita was still standing in the middle of the floor naked from the waist down. I approached one of the other ladies seated in a chair by the nurses' office. God had told me to keep lonely people company. She seemed friendly when I introduced myself, but she said little.

"Why are you here?" I asked.

"Because I'm trying to lose a few pounds."

"And have you lost any?"

"Some; I was also taking weight-reducing pills."

"Did they work?"

"For a time."

"Does anyone ever come to visit you?"

"Never."

I bounced over to another woman. God, it was hard—this task of cheering everyone up. I couldn't wait until

Chris arrived with the word that my mission was accomplished and I could go home. In the meantime, I saw various patients being called into the nurses' office for a chat with some man who looked Chinese. I also heard them paging Dr. Wing, although the nurse had already told me that they didn't page doctors.

Before I could approach my next subject, I was called into the nurses' office. I was told to sit down and talk to the doctor.

"Are you Dr. Wing? I've heard them paging him all night. Do I have to sleep in a separate room tonight? My husband is coming to get me out of here today. My mission is accomplished."

"What mission?"

"Doctor, I'm smarter than that. If I told you why I came here, why I put up with all this, you wouldn't let me out of here for the rest of my days. I see my friends here and so I must act like them to let them know that they aren't alone."

And with that, I stood up on my chair and unzipped my dress. I had nothing on underneath. The doctor watched calmly while it fell down about my waist.

I continued: "See, you put me in a place like this and you expect me to act better than the rest of the patients. Doctor, if I have to stay here, I have to act like the rest of them in order to survive. If you leave me alone at night with the rest of the patients, what do you expect? I have no other model to go by. The only thing that makes a difference between Rita and me is that I was a virgin before I got married and she's been a slut all her life. Hi, Rita!" I waved my hand so that Rita could see me through the glass window that separated the nurses' office from the lobby, then I went on. "Put Rita and me together and I have to act as though I were her friend. I have to listen to her, even though in the outside world I wouldn't look at her twice on the street. I don't know who to trust in this place. The nurses treat me like a two-year-old although I've probably had more education than any of them. What do you expect other than that I adapt to my situation?"

"Mrs. Spaight, you can trust me. I'm glad to see you are putting your dress back on. It's a good sign."

After I had zipped up my dress and taken a seat in the chair next to his desk, I said, "No, Doctor, I can't trust anyone in this place. You presume that I'm nuts without asking me what I'm thinking and you treat me like a child. If you had been here to ask me what I was thinking last night and why I was acting out, I probably wouldn't have ended up in a padded cell or in the octopus, wetting my bed and vomiting even though I called for help. Do you want me well or do you want me to be a passive vegetable?"

Chris came that afternoon but not before I attempted another escape. It was almost lunchtime, and I had wandered down the hall and somehow managed to take the wrong elevator. I thought this was the escape route that I was looking for. But it wasn't. It was just another padded elevator and it led to the men's ward. I approached the first soul I found.

"Lady, what are you doing here?"

"I'm looking for a way out. God told me that there was a way out. You don't understand. I was only supposed to stay here for a day, and they have things all mixed up. So I thought that this elevator would lead me to safety."

"Lady, there is no safety in this place. It's not that exciting, either. You're the most exciting thing that's happened to me all day."

"That's not saying very much."

"When you've been separated from your wife and family for so long, any female is exciting. But I think I'd better take you to the main desk. You don't belong on this ward. The only women on this ward are the nurses and a few attendants."

"Well, I don't really want to go back where I came from. You see, I was sent on a mission to visit everyone in the hospital."

"They don't like that. Here's the night attendant."

The attendant approached me. "My dear, what are you doing on this floor?"

"I don't know. You see I was supposed to be released today, and since my husband didn't come to get me, I thought I would meet him on the outside."

At this time I could hear the crowds outside clapping and shouting for me to come out. The television cameras were waiting. Eda, come out. You've done it! You've stayed the whole night. I could see the lights outside. There was a welcoming committee—all the people who had witnessed my stay in that terrible place were now applauding my courage.

The voice of the attendant interrupted the applause. "Come with me. I'll take you back to your proper ward. You don't belong here."

"But there's some mistake. I'm not supposed to go back to the ward. There's been some terrible mixup. I'm supposed to leave today. Everyone is waiting for me on the outside."

"You'll have to discuss that with the nurse on your ward."

"Honest, you could die in this place from an administrative mixup. All right, I'll go back to the ward. But I want to know where my husband is. He was supposed to be here hours ago. Nobody talks about him coming to see me."

By this time the attendant and I were on the elevator. We journeyed through endless corridors of gray cement until we finally arrived at my ward. The nurse at the desk looked up from behind her horn-rimmed glasses.

"Oh, Mrs. Spaight, have you been wandering off again to points unknown? You're supposed to stay on this ward."

"I want to see my husband. I'm supposed to go home today. No one talks about him coming to see me."

"Mrs. Spaight, why don't you go to lunch? You only have five minutes before the line closes."

"When is he coming?"

"Why don't you join the other patients at lunch?"

"I'm not a patient. It was all a joke. Don't you understand? I'm supposed to be released today. If Chris doesn't come for me, I'm supposed to meet him at the entrance. I'll go to lunch."

"Yes, and after that you're supposed to take your pill."

I went to lunch, but I wasn't hungry. I picked at my food. Why wouldn't anyone mention Chris? Why wouldn't they tell me if he was coming? I couldn't spend another day in this place.

After lunch I was sleepy, but there was a man who came up and wanted to talk to me. He was elderly, kind, and seemed to know Papa. He wore a lab jacket and ushered me into a separate room.

"Mrs. Spaight, I want to talk to you."

"About what? If I stay any longer in this place, I'm sure I won't know what I'm talking about."

"Just sit down and rest. The doctor who speaks Spanish sent me. He was interested in your case."

It made no sense to me. My head was buzzing, and when I glanced out of the window, I could see the crowd waiting for me on the outside. They were clapping and yelling for me to come out.

My interviewer continued: "Why don't you tell me the whole story?"

"What is there to tell you? I loved my father and my mother, and I was a good student in school. I lived on amphetamines before that, but now I've quit."

"Then you are a lawyer."

"Yes."

"Are you a member of the bar?"

"No. Not here. I wrote to the Supreme Court of New York expressing my ideas on the bar exam and returned my ticket of admission to the exam. Everyone, from my father on down to my husband, disapproved. I'm too far ahead of the times. People aren't ready for me or my ideas. They spell revolution. Oh, no, I'm not going to say what I thought at the time or what I now think."

"You're an intelligent person. I understand that you speak fluent Spanish."

"And Portuguese and Italian and French and English. But I'm not intelligent—not when all it does for me is set me up in an octopus and relegate me to the level of a two-year-old in the eyes of your nurses. As far as they're concerned, I had better take my pills, eat the meals, and go to sleep on time. I'm going to forget what I know and think, and then maybe I'll get out of here."

"What does your father do?"

"He's a surgeon in Syracuse, New York."

"Is that how you got the amphetamines?"

"Sure. I used to take a bunch of blank prescriptions and write out #200 Preludin 25 mg. T.I.D. Refills x 4."

"What do you think of your father?"

"I think he's a better doctor than any of the doctors I've met here. He answered a call day or night—whenever his patients wanted him, he was there. He never would leave them so long that they had to sleep in their own urine and vomit and get sick the next day. He cared for his patients all the time. That's why they didn't want anyone else. The doctors here are all over the place. You don't see them from one day to the next. They listen, but they don't really care. I saw one writing down on his notepad while I was talking: paranoid schizophrenic, drug-induced, hallucinating in the auditory and visual spheres! It's not nice to write such things about me. I'm human."

"Were you ever in any other hospital?"

"Yes. Three years ago. I did the same thing. I thought I might have changed."

"How long were you in the other hospital?"

"About six months."

"Did you like it?"

"There was something to do all the time. We had regular gym sessions, painting sessions, sewing sessions, cooking sessions, music sessions. I talked much less to the patients when I got well and I devoted all my time to these skills."

"Are you sick now?"

"No. I just have a few strange theories that I think I had better annihilate."

"You're married. Are you happy?"

"Not now, I'm not with my husband. I've never been separated from him and put in a place like this. I want him to take me out of here."

"Do you want to go to another hospital?"

"Like this? Hell no. I can't stand the place. No place in the world could be as bad as this place or as dangerous. I've been scared out of my senses ever since I arrived. You leave the patients unattended at night. A night nurse comes around every few hours. One of the patients could kill another patient in the meantime. I may be nuts but I'm not blind to my own safety."

"Mrs. Spaight, if we could transfer you to another hospital, would you like it better?"

"What do I need a hospital for? I'm not sick."

"You need a rest then."

"I want to see my husband and I want to hear what he says. He's supposed to pick me up today."

"I'll see what I can do, Mrs. Spaight."

"You'd better hurry. People are waiting for me on the outside—important people. People who know what this whole joke is about."

When I left the small conference room, I went straight to the lobby. Chris was there waiting for me. The rest of the patients eyed him curiously. There were few other visitors. Chris looked worried and preoccupied.

"Chris, I'm supposed to leave today. Didn't you come to take me home?"

"Eda, it took me hours just to get in and see you. I had to wait four hours just to see a doctor downstairs."

At this point, Rita came over and stood close to Chris. I was used to her makeup, but Chris wasn't.

"Chris, I want to introduce you to some of my friends—some of the people that I've met here."

"But, Eda, I want to talk to you."

"Well, as long as I won't be leaving today, you might as well get acquainted. I didn't know that my mission in this place was going to last longer than a day."

"Eda, I'm trying to get you out of here as fast as possible."

"Chris, let's put the puzzle together. I haven't had anyone help me put the puzzle together. Let's let Rita help us."

We sat down at the table and confronted the pile of

jagged pieces, trying, one by one, to fit them into the flat pattern of a country landscape that was slowly emerging.

"Chris, there's nothing much to do here but sit and talk and eat. There aren't very many people to talk to, other than Betty and Rita. I walk the halls a lot. I get very restless. I don't talk about my ideas anymore because the more I talk the longer I'm going to stay. I'm going to annihilate all my ideas, Chris."

"Eda, I don't want you to stay here."

"Why not, Chris? I'm among friends."

At this point Rita stopped assembling the pieces of the puzzle. She stared at Chris and smiled. Then she brushed the hair away from her painted face, screamed, and slid the puzzle onto the floor into three hundred pieces. Chris was startled, but I didn't pay any attention and continued my conversation.

"Chris, if I have to show the rest of the world that I'm right, that I have no fears—even to the point of entering a mental institution and being the only sane person—if that's the only way that I can prove my cause, if that's the sacrifice that's required of a thinking person in a world full of schmucks, then I'm happy to stay right here."

"Don't you want to come home?"

"I told you that people are waiting for me on the outside, that I've done a very brave thing—something that I think Papa wouldn't even dare to do. You're the only one who has faith in me, and I'll prove that it was all worth it. I love you, Chris, and I want to come home. But I have a mission to be completed. So far, I haven't convinced anyone of the value of it. But I don't care. They poisoned Socrates for finding out the truth. Today when you're an innovator, they lock you up. I'm willing to pay the price."

"Eda, this isn't the place for you. I'm going to get you out of here if it's the last thing I do."

"Mr. Spaight, visiting time is over."

"Chris, I love you. Will you come to see me again? When will you get me out of here?"

I roamed aimlessly through the halls after Chris's visit. Locked up in a living hell where there was no difference between the passing of each hour, or the passing of days, Chris's visit had an effect. It brought memories of home. Chris loved me. It meant more than all the psychotherapy in the world. Even though he didn't understand, he felt. The doctors and nurses were trained not to feel. Any doctor who took the state hospital with him at night might remain a permanent resident of the place. I couldn't blame them. Hell, I was there because no one in the real world understood my case.

After pacing the halls for an hour, I came back into the main room. I looked up at the bars on the high windows. I looked at the gray cement-block walls of the state fortress and started talking out loud, "God, why have you abandoned me? I'm your child Eda. Please, if I have to stay in this place, give me a sign that you're with me."

I looked up at the window again and saw a dove. "Rita. He's here. God hasn't left me. I asked for a sign, and He sent me one. Look up at the window. See the dove—the sign of peace, the sign of heaven."

I went over to the old lady in the chair. Rita tried to hold me back. "Get away from her, Eda, everyone has told you that she's dangerous." I wrenched out of Rita's grasp and went over to the old lady.

"Do you see God? God is at the window."

She looked at me and smiled, "You Italian?"

"Yes."

"You Sicilian?"

"Yes."

"I Sicilian. I Vincincina. Ha! Ha! Ha!" Vincincina began to laugh. It was a wild, hysterical, crying laughter. She continued: "You pretty young Sicilian girl. Ha! Ha! Ha! I used to be like you. Get away from me before I bite your hand off. Ha! Ha! Ha!"

I walked away while Vincincina was still laughing and crying and laughing.

I was allowed to spend that night in the regular ward with the rest of the patients. Before going to bed, I was given a stiff dosage of Thorazine. It kept me groggy and passive the next day. Every time the drug started to wear off, I felt that they were intentionally killing me, sapping me of my strength and beating me down so that I couldn't explain my cause or think clearly. I was becoming like the rest of the inmates—slow, passive, docile, and sleepy. I felt more discouraged, more lonely, more abandoned by the world outside.

The nurses soon commented on my lack of activity. As in the navy hospital, I found sleep a pleasant escape, a way of passing the time. I fussed with the puzzle in the afternoon or gazed out of the window. I waited for Chris.

Two days passed. I was moping around the halls one day when suddenly I thought I was seeing things. It was Mom! Holy wow-now-green bananas! Mom! And she was with Chris! I started running down the hall with my arms outstretched. I couldn't run fast enough. Tears were streaming down my face! "Mama! Mama Franchi. Why did you come? Is it time to take me home? Mama! Take me out of this place." The nurses winced as I went dashing past them. I didn't see them. Only I saw Mom.

Mom was dressed in a light blue knit suit. Her blue-white hair was crisply styled under a small blue veil. She looked stunning. I grabbed her and hugged her. "Mama, I'm Eda. Help me. Don't cry, Mom. I'm dirty and look awful. I swear I'm okay, Mom; wipe those tears away. If you cry, I'll start to cry and I'm really okay. I just want to get the hell out of here."

Chris said that I would leave the hospital that day. "I'm going home. I can't believe it. I knew that someone would soon realize that it was all a horrible mistake. I'm not sick. I told you that someone would see the light."

The nurses came up to me. "Mrs. Spaight, come with me," one of them said. "I want you to come into the room at the end of the hall."

"What for? I haven't done a goddamn thing in the last two days and I'm going home. Okay, so I ran down the hall when I saw Mom. I guess the rules here don't allow for excitement when your mother comes? Or maybe you don't like your mother as much as I do mine. Maybe your mother isn't as nice as mine. My mother's beautiful."

"Come into the room, Mrs. Spaight, and lie down on the bed. If you're good, this needle won't hurt."

"If you know how to give it properly, it won't hurt. As long as I'm leaving this afternoon, nothing matters. Give me the needle."

"We'll be sorry to see you go."

"Don't say that. Why compound a felony? I was just another pain in the neck, another bothersome nut that you had to control. Lying doesn't make my departure that much sweeter."

"Mrs. Spaight, we care about our patients, as long as they behave and obey."

"Come off it—as long as they do what they are told and as long as they don't bother you, they're good patients. You can give me all the needles in the world, but you can't convince me that you're sincere. Just take a tip from a nutty lawyer who's leaving. Don't treat these people like two-year-olds and maybe they'll surprise you by not acting like two-year-olds. It's impossible for some —like Vincincina who's too far gone—but it shouldn't be the story with everyone."

"Come into the bathroom, Mrs. Spaight. We're going to get you all cleaned up for your departure."

"I haven't taken a bath since I came here. That urine is still on my legs although I managed to get most of the vomit out of my hair. Without attendants, I was afraid. Someone might forcefully put me under. Have they cleaned up the bathroom? There's a consistent practice of missing the toilet and going on the floor."

"You sound bitter."

"No. Just civilized, that's all. However you diagnose my illness, it certainly isn't lack of observation."

That afternoon I was cleaned, dressed, and human again. When I walked out of the hospital, I thought I was going home. The crowds were no longer waiting, only Chris and Mom.

"Where are we off to?" I asked.

Mom looked tired.

"Where's Papa?"

"He didn't come, Eda. He'll come to see you later."

"At home?"

"No, Eda, we're going to another hospital."

"Oh, God! You didn't tell me that the mission wasn't finished. I have to go to every hospital in the state and visit all the patients before I can be released from this ominous task."

"Eda, what are you talking about?"

"It's okay. I just didn't realize the magnitude of my duties."

"We're going to take you to a place where you'll get proper care."

"But, Mom, Chris said that I could get over drugs by staying at home."

"We're taking you to Easton Park. It's a much better place. Dr. Liebowitz recommended it."

"I'm not really sick, but if you think that I should visit, it should be interesting."

"We love you, Eda, we're doing this for your own good so that you'll soon be well."

"But I'm not sick. Chris says there's nothing the matter with me. I have my theories, but as I told Chris, I was going to annihilate them."

Soon we arrived at the entrance to Easton Park Hospital. It was modern and sterile. It was everything that a private hospital could be without being homey. I had been assigned to "T" ward. Mom and Chris had a brief discussion with the doctor and then he wanted to see me.

"Mrs. Spaight, my name is Dr. Stein. Will you please come with me?"

We walked into one of the doctor's offices and sat down.

"Do you know why you're here, Mrs. Spaight?"

"No."

I was still under the impression that it was my duty to visit all the hospitals in the area. The doctor had convinced these people that they were sick. But I had learned my lesson from the state mental hospital. No matter how the doctors wanted to help me, I basically didn't trust them. Their purpose was to reduce me to the stagnation that was normalcy. I remained passive during the interview and revealed as little about myself as possible. I had no idea why I was in the hospital at all. But the Romans had crucified Christ for less reason than that. I knew that my analogies to occurrences in the Bible would make no sense to Dr. Stein or any other doctor. Doctors just didn't believe in the Bible. They worried about the self rather than the sacrifice of self, which was my basic philosophy. The interview continued.

"Then as far as you're concerned, Mrs. Spaight, there's nothing wrong with you."

"I'm in the process of annihilating anything that is."

"Good."

"I knew that you would say that."

"Why?"

"Simple; if I didn't, I wouldn't be able to get out of here."

"Do you like me, Mrs. Spaight?"

"I don't even know you. How can I like you?"

"Do you like doctors?"

"Generally, no. I like my father and he's a doctor. The rest of the doctors are usually impressed with the fact that they're doctors, just like lawyers are impressed being lawyers, even though they have no more brains or ambition than the average person. Doctors are a bunch of stuffed shirts. They get a bigger kick out of classifying me as a passive aggressive personality than wondering what I'm really like."

"Do you know what you're really like?"

"No, and I don't care. I just don't fit into any of the categories that you'd like to fit me into."

"Would you like to stay here for a few days?"

"Why?"

"So that we can hear what you have to say and what you think."

"I'm not going to tell you that. I'd really prefer to go home and live with my husband. I don't like hospitals."

"No one likes hospitals, Mrs. Spaight, but Easton Park can help you."

"Thanks, I didn't know I needed the help."

"Our ward is very new. We experiment a lot."

"Do you give people needles at night and put them in

an octopus? Do you lock them up? I really didn't intend to stay the whole night."

I didn't tell the doctor during the interview, or any of the nurses, about my delusions. I had just finished reading Ayn Rand's book *Atlas Shrugged* where all the geniuses of society had retreated to an unknown location in order to carry on their creative arts. Since Dr. Stein was very attractive and well dressed and since all the other patients were dressed in ordinary clothes, I immediately assumed that I had found the artist's colony described in the book. Everyone that I talked to on the ward had his specific talent. Most of the patients equaled or exceeded me in intelligence, so I assumed that they were all authors or movie actors. I was finally where I belonged. The group looked offbeat and intellectual. Maybe I had arrived at the right spot.

The doctor continued talking. But he was no longer a doctor. He was a Hollywood producer.

"Mrs. Spaight, what is your first name? May I call you by your first name?"

"Certainly. People call me Eda."

"Would you like to stay for lunch?"

"What about Chris and Mom?"

"They'll come to see you after lunch. I'd just like you to get acquainted. Here, meet Brenda Devins. Mrs. Devins will take care of you and introduce you around."

Mrs. Devins was a nurse, but to me she was another movie star acting the part of a nurse. And she wasn't like the nurses at State; she was human.

Brenda Devins and I walked into the lobby where the guests were still mingling with the patients. I couldn't tell the difference. Everyone seemed so friendly.

A few of the patients came over and introduced themselves. "Hey, girl, what's your name? I'm Jim. Welcome to our community. This is Drew and that's Todd."

"I'm not staying long. I just came for a visit."

"Too bad, girl. You turn me on all over. Hey, Drew, I want to play my guitar for this chick."

"Man, play it cool, man. You're supposed to be released in a week."

"No. I'm telling you the truth, Drew. She's sexy. I don't care how sick she is. Your name's Eda. Come, Eda, would you like to hear me play my guitar? We've got time before lunch. Dave also plays the guitar and accompanies me. Hey, Agnes, gather round. We're going to have a little music."

Agnes was a Ph.D. candidate at Columbia who had just had a baby. The baby was with her in the hospital, and her former husband was there visiting.

Jimmy played loud and clear. He played "House of the Rising Sun," then "King of the Road." Then he played some love ballads that he had composed himself.

As I sat listening, I smiled at Jimmy. He winked and blew me a kiss. I liked these people immediately. They were my kind of people. They accepted my theories when I talked and didn't threaten me. Then I met Herby, short for Herbert. Herby stood still and didn't say anything.

The attendants were so talented that it never dawned on me that they were there to watch and control. Dave, one of the male attendants, played the guitar and sang in several languages. He charmed Mom immediately.

After lunch, I asked Dr. Stein when I was going to be taken on a tour of the rest of the hospital. It was my time to bring cheer to the rest of the wards. My suitcase was dropped off in a room without incident.

In the meantime, my blood pressure was taken, and Brenda introduced me to some more patients.

Milly was a short, round, roly-poly girl who wore a lot of eye makeup and looked Spanish. She must play minor roles in the films that the colony produced. More than half the patients played the guitar, sang, and had gone to college. Everyone told me that Herby was Phi Beta Kappa.

Everything in this new hospital was so open. The doors were open. There were no locks on the bedrooms. I had no idea that I was going to stay at this delightful playground of actors and actresses until they all became nurses and patients—sick people—for well over six months. My first attempt at escape that first night proved that I had lost all touch with reality.

When five o'clock came, Chris and Mom departed. I misunderstood the situation entirely and approached Dr. Stein immediately.

"But, Doctor, I'm supposed to go with them. We only came to the colony for a visit."

"Eda, don't you like this place?"

"Sure I like the place. But you don't understand. It's not my place. The people are lovely; they're different from the last place. But I'm not under contract. What I'm doing is purely out of charity."

At this time the lights came on. The cameras were again focusing on my conversation with the doctor. He was terribly busy with the phones, the nurses, and me. It was almost dinnertime and the nurses were ringing bells to get the patients in to dinner. It was just like on television. We were really under the cameras and really under the lights. Dr. Stein told me that it was the dinner hour and that Chris would be back to see me the next day. Chris was still in the navy, so it was a two-hour commute each way between the base and the hospital. He made the trip every day and never complained about the long hours.

That night at dinner, I met more patients and more attendants. I sat and kidded with Dave, the black attendant. He sang and played the guitar, and I accompanied him in Italian. During all this time the stage lights were blazing in my eyes. When dinner with the patients was over, it was time for me to leave the colony and go home.

Before dinner I had spied a sign that read "Exit." I assumed that this was the back exit from the stage and didn't understand why no one was leaving on cue. I approached Marie, one of the night attendants, and inquired: "But the show is over, isn't it?"

"The dinner show, yes; we have wonderful food around here."

"But I must leave. I spoke to the doctor earlier about leaving. He asked me to stay for a few days, but I've changed my mind."

"But, Eda, you just came. Besides, we have a short meeting tonight after visiting hours and it's almost time to take your blood pressure. Come, I'll wait in line with you. See, everyone is lining up to have their blood pressure taken."

"But I wasn't meant to stay. I'm an actress."

"And this is the stage."

"Right. And now I must go home to keep my husband company."

With that last statement I made one mad dash down the hall, through the dining room to the sign that read "Exit." Damn, the door was locked. There must be a stairway behind it that led all the way down and out of the hospital. Dave was close at my heels.

"Eda, what are you trying to do?"

Soon Dr. Stein was behind Dave. The lights were flashing again, so that I knew we were on television. Dr. Stein wrenched me away from the door.

"Eda, I want to talk to you."

"I don't want to talk. I want to get out of here. You said that I could leave anytime I wished."

"I want to talk to you in my private office."

Since I felt this was still part of the television program, I took his hand and went into the office. When we were inside, he asked me to sit down.

"Eda, you're not going to make it through the meeting tonight unless I give you something to calm you down. You're way up. Way up there."

"I know. Things are moving awfully fast. I get the impression that I'm causing a lot of trouble when I don't intend to. At the last place, they locked me in a padded cell and put me in an octopus where I shit in my bed. I vomited and had to sleep in it all night."

"We don't do that here. Eda, are you harmless? Do I have your word?"

"I'm harmless and incoherent. Lights keep flashing and mixing me up."

"I'm going to try some medication that will make you feel more at ease while you're here. Will you take it right now?"

"Is it a needle? I don't want a needle."

"I won't give you a needle if you don't want it."

"I don't want it."

"Then I'll give you some liquid. You're a very puzzling case and I'm going to try different drugs on you and ask you how they make you feel. I want a truthful answer."

I left the doctor's office and took the liquid Thorazine from Brenda. Soon the lights faded away, and I was more or less carried into the meeting. I caught a few of the words. The patients welcomed me to the colony and attempted to explain the system. Since I wasn't staying, I took the whole thing as inapplicable. These people were talking about a long-term commitment. They were talking of getting better when I never felt better.

The system itself consisted of steps on a ladder. When you were on the bottom rung, as I was, you were escorted throughout the ward under the careful eyes of a nurse. As you calmed down and felt better, you were escorted around by a "buddy"—another patient who was soon to be discharged. The next step you were on your own but had to stay within the limits of the ward. You were given little responsibility other than to attend all the meetings and conferences. Step four was that of monitor. As a monitor you started to organize things. You got up at six thirty to attend the nurses' morning reports on all the patients. You called all the patients to the meetings and took care of minor details, like organizing the chairs and greeting parents. You summoned the patients to all the meals and made sure that everyone was accounted for and that all the rooms were neat and orderly for inspection. You made sure . . . etc., etc.

It took me four months to become a monitor, and I was a monitor with pride. But my initial impression was that these people couldn't mean what they were saying or else that it didn't apply to me. I was only there as a guest, so I decided to leave. I was bored and restless. Brenda tried to hold me back.

"Eda, you can't leave. The meeting isn't over."

"Brenda, I have to go to the bathroom. I have to get up and go somewhere. What are they talking about anyway? None of it applies to me. I have to go and visit the other wards. The doctor promised me."

"Eda, after the meeting you can go to bed like most of the other people or you can watch TV. Try to take an interest in other people's problems. That's what we're all here for."

As we walked out of the meeting and sat in an empty bedroom, I continued: "I can't take an interest in these people's problems. God has told me to—yes—but I'm not Jesus Christ. Nor am I Job. I don't take things with ease. Next week I plan to go to Washington and plead my case about the bar exam. The whole thing was so unfair. I have to talk to Eric Sevareid and uproot the whole system. It's so studded with normalcy and give-in-ism. I make up my own words as I go along because nothing else seems to fit. Don't you understand? I'm fighting a cause and I guess that's why I'm here. People aren't supposed to fight causes anymore. I'm here because that's what the rest of society has done to me. They've crucified me just like they crucified Christ. For what? For having ideas different from anyone else's and the guts to risk anything to do something about it. I think I'll have a soda and another pill. I really can't go back to the meeting and I don't know what to do with myself."

"Eda, you must talk to the other patients. They can be very helpful. They're going through the same thing that you're going through now."

"Brenda, I hear music. Look. The meeting's over and Jimmy's playing the guitar."

Jimmy was playing his guitar and it sounded beautiful. Tonight he was playing love songs and sad songs, playing them loudly and spiritedly. As he saw me join the group, he started to play my favorite, "House of the Rising Sun." I made Jimmy play it three times that night and later told him that I needed to learn the words—that it really meant something to me.

"Hey, doll, you're really turned on."

"I love your music, Jimmy. I'm young and alive. I don't want to die in this place. I told you that I believe in a perfect circle, that when you have turned around and twisted back on yourself only then are you perfect."

"I understand you, baby, but you're rapping."

"What's that?"

"You'll understand, but not now. Alix will tell you. She used to rap a lot."

Alix approached me. She was a long, tall, unkempt girl who had a pockmarked face, but nonetheless potential good looks if she would only take care of herself. But Alix only cared about all the people she took under her wing. I was one of them.

"Are you uptight, kid? You can talk to me. I know what it's like."

"Oh, really, no. I'm not uptight. I'm here for a visit. I'm only staying a few days."

"Come on. What did you take? Heroin?"

"No. Just amphetamines, barbiturates, antidepressants, tranquilizers and codeine—the usual run-of-the-mill pill stuff."

"You'll come down soon. Did you enjoy the meeting tonight?"

"No, I was bored. I couldn't sit still that long."

"You're going to have to learn to take an interest in what's happening to all of us. We're like in it together."

"How long have you been here?"

"Eight months. I'll show you around when you're up to it. Right now I suggest that you go to bed. It's past midnight."

"Really, I'm not tired."

"You will be. They don't keep you sitting here on your ass all day like they do at State. I know. I came from there."

"Join me for a soda before I go to bed."

My bed was the one closest to the door where Dave, the attendant, watched over me. It had bars on both sides but it was comfortable, so I didn't complain. Dave was sympathetic as I crawled into bed.

"Cheer up, Eda. You have a big day ahead of you tomorrow."

"Dave, Alix told me that they don't let you take naps."

"Maybe twenty minutes after lunch if you can fit it in after your blood pressure is taken."

I crawled into bed. The pills that Dr. Stein prescribed

started to take effect, but they weren't strong enough to dispel the nightmares that started that night. I had gone to bed around one o'clock and found myself in the midst of a frozen dream at about three. I woke up Dave. He had dozed off, reading in the chair outside the room.

"Dave. I've got to go to the bathroom and then I've got to talk to you."

I never made it. Dave had to find a female to take me to the bathroom. I couldn't control myself and went running down the hall. As I ran, my bladder let loose and the urine started to trickle down my legs.

I shouted to myself. Oh, shit! This is what it's like to go off pills. I'm like an animal. I dream half of the day and I'm unhappy. The rest of the time, I don't know who the hell I am or where I'm going in this place. I hate myself. I hate life. I don't want to die and go back to normalcy. The same old crap day in and day out. The same old worry about putting on weight.

My thoughts gave way and I ended up sobbing in the bathroom. Marie, the woman attendant, was waiting outside. I didn't want to face her. I didn't want to face anyone while in the depths of such despair. I meekly washed myself off and returned with Marie to talk to Dave. As I walked down the corridor wiping my eyes, he asked: "Had a rough time so far?"

"I don't know what I'm doing here. I'd feel safer trying to get over this at home."

"You'd be no better on the outside."

"No, but at least I'd be convinced that I belonged there. This is my second time. What happens to me? My family comes here and says, 'Poor Eda, you're sick. You need to take a rest. You shouldn't push yourself so hard.' Then when I was at school nothing was said except to do my best. But it's still the same old story. Eda, you should relax. All my life my father busted his ass to get somewhere, and he did. Then he's got the nerve to tell me—his own flesh and blood—to take it easy. Do you know what that did to me? It made me work all the harder. And all the thanks I got for all that trying was a pat on the head and the compliment that I was Papa Franchi's little girl. Hell of a way to reach twenty-five and be a lawyer."

"Eda, tell me about your nightmare. That's what you wanted to talk about—wasn't it?"

"Well, I was asleep and all of a sudden pythons started swarming around me. I hate snakes and worms to begin with. Snakes make me cringe. They kept coming closer and they were so slimy, I could feel them touch me. There was no relief. Usually, I wake up, but this time I didn't wake up. They kept on with their ugly tongues coming out at me until I began to sweat. That's when I woke up and had to go to the bathroom. I'm weary and I'm afraid to go back to bed. I'm afraid they'll come back."

"Do you want a pill to go to sleep? You won't be able to sleep tomorrow and the night nurse won't give you pills after four in the morning."

"I want a pill, even though Chris says that I can do it without pills. I don't want any more snakes. I don't want any more frozen dreams. I don't want any more worms."

"Do you want to talk to the nurse?"

"No. How can I tell her I'm so uptight that I need something to get some rest? You know I don't like sleep. It's a waste of time. I haven't had a good night's sleep in three years. Instead I've stayed awake to study and work."

"Eda, come into the other room. I'll play my guitar. There's nothing like music to calm the nerves."

As we walked into the lobby, I saw Jimmy in the doorway of his room. I didn't look at him as we passed. I was ashamed. But he touched my arm. "Eda," he said.

"I'm dying, man. Leave me alone. I just crapped all over myself."

"Eda, I've been here nine months. I used to shoot up the hard stuff. So did Milly, Drew, and Alix. Now, I'm going back to Virginia. It's worth it, girl. Stick it out. You've got a long road to travel. I'll play for you if it makes life easier. I'll play until I leave."

The next morning I was up at six o'clock. I had been told not to eat anything since my blood sample would be taken that morning.

I asked the nurse: "Where's Brenda Devins? The doctor said no needles and now this morning he wants to use a needle. I want to talk to Brenda, my escort."

"Brenda will be in soon, Eda. They take blood tests once a week. There'll be others."

"But I'll be the first. I want to get it over with."

"Have you always been so afraid of needles?"

"Yes. I hate needles. That's why I never shot up."

I walked down the hall and stood in line. So far I was the only one. But I was scared. Even since Hamden State where the unexpected was the norm, I approached each new project with mixed feelings of fear and desperation. With pills I had been able to manage my own life. Now everyone else was telling me how and what to do. I felt weak. I felt the pain of not knowing and having to turn to professional strangers. Soon other patients gathered in the line.

"Does it hurt?" I wanted to know.

Alix was there. "Yes, it hurts for a minute or two. Never hurt me because I used to shoot up anyway. It hurts if he can't find the right vein. These interns, you know, they act as if they're God right off the bat and can solve the world's problems."

The intern arrived. He was one of the doctors that I'd seen on the night rounds. He went in and prepared the small lab room.

I walked in cheerfully and he smiled. "Well, I see that we have a new patient."

"That was the wrong thing to say, Doctor. As far as I know, I'm only here for a visit."

"All right, then we have a new visitor. Put your arm out straight and clench your fist, please."

He put the tourniquet around my arm. I couldn't look.

"What's your name?"

"Eda Franchi Spaight. Tell me when it's all over with."

I felt the needle puncture the outer surface of the skin, and then the pain stopped.

"Aren't you going to tell me that I'm a brave girl like my papa used to tell me?"

The doctor looked puzzled.

"How old did you say you are, Eda?"

"Twenty-five."

"And your father still talks to you like that?"

"All the time and especially when I take a needle."

After the bloodletting, I went into the dining room. Brenda was again assigned to me for the day. I told her about the night before and my nightmares. I felt so strange in the place and I had the bad habit of rapping—that is talking to everyone about everything all at once. To me it all made sense, but to everyone else I was a sterling case, pegged for at least a six-month stay at Easton Park.

I hadn't had my morning pill and I was restless. I had made friends with the kitchen help and eagerly accepted the job of helping Lucy, the cook, set up the tables for breakfast. Everyone else was in the morning fog that follows the heavy dosage of tranquilizers necessary for prolonged hospitalization. Since I hated food and was off my safety catch of amphetamines, I ate very little breakfast. Alix told me that everyone gains weight sitting around in the hospital. When I got on the scales that morning, I weighed 132 pounds. Now I had to worry about everything that I ate as well as the dosage of tranquilizers that they were pounding into me night and day. I had stayed on amphetamines because of my diabolical concern with calories. In college it had always been boom or bust. I was either on a starvation diet or gorging myself and then taking a raw egg to barf it up. On amphetamines, the whole thing had been controlled. I was active and never had the worries of a normal human being who's afraid that they can't or won't control themselves. Now Aunt Gabriella was before my eyes asking me: "Why you no *mangia*? Eda, why you no *mangia*?"

After breakfast I met Gwen. Gwen was my ideal. She didn't have a figure. She was too thin to have one, and the doctors had told Gwen that if she didn't eat, she'd end up in State. Gwen didn't want to eat. Gwen was five feet six inches and weighed only ninety-four pounds. If she ever wanted to leave Easton Park, Gwen had to gain ten pounds.

Gwen and I hung around a lot together during those days. She never bothered to try and figure me out like so many of the other patients had. She accepted me as I was, maybe because her problems were the same as mine. Something was bugging the hell out of her, but she took it out on the scales. I would tell Gwen that I wasn't concerned with banalities like eating. I was concerned with higher things, the ideas that normal people don't bother with, that thinkers of my century declined to talk about.

But when I finished, Gwen looked sad. "Eda, don't rot away in this place for the sake of ideas. You don't want to stay here forever. I've been here almost three months and I'm so bored with the place I could scream."

"Why did you come here in the first place?"

"Because I wasn't eating at home. I only weighed eighty pounds, and my parents were worried about me."

Alix came into the room. Her hair was unkempt as usual, and she had just finished recording the blood pressures. "Eda, Brenda is looking for you. You forgot. You're not supposed to go anywhere without a nurse. Cheer up. You'll soon make it to the point where you're assigned a buddy."

"So, I'm supposed to find Brenda?"

"No, she'll find you, and don't worry. It will go down on your record."

"Alix, I can't figure out why you and Gwen want to leave the place. I think it's great. You get someone to talk to all day long and they treat you like a human being."

"You've been here two days. Wait until the months start to drag on and all you have to look forward to is going home to your parents," Alix said. "Hell, I was happier wigging out in Ashbury. You're still in the highs, kid. Wait until you come down."

Brenda soon found me and reminded me to keep in touch. After breakfast, we had another meeting. This time the patients met alone, led by Milly, the acting chairman. The discussion started out with reports of each buddy about the person that they were escorting and was followed by a direct question-and-answer session between the chairman and particular patients regarding their progress. There were about thirty patients, so the meeting was bound to be long and involved.

Milly asked Inga, a sweet old German lady who had a hearing aid, how she was feeling.

"I can't hear you. This contraption that they gave me for my ear doesn't work. I can't hear you."

"Inga, you've been saying that for a month, but there's nothing wrong with your hearing."

I said to myself, *Milly's right. Inga's just telling herself that.*

"Inga, you have to try," Milly continued. "If you don't, you'll never hear again."

Inga answered in a heavy German accent. "But I don't understand what you're saying. You have to speak more clearly."

Milly got impatient. She was always impatient and bossy. I was afraid to cross her. She seemed so strong in comparison to me.

Suddenly Milly turned to me. "Eda, how do you feel?"

"I don't feel. Everyone's been asking me how I feel, and I've been trying to tell you that the mind is the most important thing in existence. I've been trying to tell you that I think. *I think, therefore I am.*"

Drew let out a yell in the back: "You tell them, baby. I've been trying to sell Lao-tzu to them for months. I see you go for the French men."

Drew had been in the hospital for months. He had been on LSD. We were very good friends in the beginning, but Drew was permanently tripped out. Acid had eaten out his mind, and desperation about his fate had rotted his core. Later, when I began to change and Drew didn't, we drifted apart.

Egged on by Drew, I continued rapping.

Alix nudged me. "You're talking far-out, kid, when you hit the unified cycle bit. It's going to ruin your chances to ditch Brenda and get a patient buddy."

I addressed Milly: "Am I free to say what I want here, or are you going to act like a court of law and convict me before I've finished the argument?"

Milly was curt. "Counselor, you aren't in a court of law. You're a mental patient. The sooner you realize that you've gone ape shit on amphetamines and downers, the sooner we'll try to help you."

"I want to leave."

"You can't. The meeting isn't over with yet."

"I don't care. I put in my application to be placed with a buddy, and you and the rest of the patients just turned me down."

"Eda, you aren't ready."

"Oh, yes, I'm ready to get the hell out of this kangaroo court and go home to my husband. He's the only one who can help me, and I was a fool for coming here in the first place. I have to leave. I can't sit still one minute longer. Drew is right, and you don't listen to him."

By this time the meeting was getting out of hand. Milly let Brenda take me for a walk so I wouldn't blow the place apart. I stomped out, accompanied by Brenda. Milly was in control and bossy as hell—just like Papa had been at home sometimes. I could hear his words ringing in my ears: "I tell you, Mother, he's nothing but a lazy bastard. Goes out and doodles the whole day and then you help him with his reading. He should be like Eda. He never did get the grades that Eda got."

"Papa, dear. I'll stand behind all my children—right or wrong."

"He's a no-good lazy bum. You've done nothing but baby him all these years. You hear me, Luci? You're nothing but a goddamn lazy no-good bum and you're upsetting your mother. You ought to be ashamed of yourself. Get the hell out of the house, boy. I don't want to see you."

"Papa Franchi, he's your son too. Don't pick on him all the time."

"Goddamnit, you bastards, I'm the boss of this house. Do you all hear me? As long as you stay under this roof, you obey me. You never listen to me. I work all day long and I have to come home to a bunch of ill-bred, goddamn bastards. I have patients who listen to me, who take my advice, and then when I come home, I'm nothing. I'm going to sell the house and leave you all."

I tore the scene out of my mind. Things were going too fast. Milly had crossed me. She couldn't be trusted anymore.

That afternoon I appeared at lunch wearing a dress with my pink slacks underneath. I braided my hair into two thin braids on each side and let the rest fall down straight. I felt that I looked Egyptian. Brenda asked me to go back to my room and take off my slacks. I told her that this was fashionable dress in the Middle Eastern countries, and besides, it was comfortable. I was going to wear the pants and the dress.

"Someday people will be wearing pants with their dresses, Brenda. I can see ahead into the future years. You say that *I'm* having a nervous breakdown. When I tell you that I'm no one, that I exist for the benefit of others, to do good for the rest of mankind, you say that I'm nuts. Explain that in terms of the United States where we care so much about the world that we can't bother with the civil unrest at home. We had damn well better. The generation gap is so wide between the stuffed-shirt rulers of this country and the actual goings-on that young people like me sit down and say: What the hell? Why not do your own thing? It's right, it's beautiful, and God is with us! I'm tired of the stagnation of everyday living, the take-it-easy-don't-kill-yourself attitude that you people encourage. I'm for living and dying with intensity, with all the fear and emotional anxiety that make up a whole person."

"Dr. Stein would like to see you," was Brenda's answer.

"Is he going to give me a shot?"

"No, he'd just like to talk to you."

Dr. Stein entered and invited me into his office. "Eda, how long can you sit still?"

"About five minutes."

"Your husband told me that you can't even tell the time of day."

"That's right. I get lost with the numbers."

"Are you comfortable with the medicine that I gave you?"

"No. People and thoughts keep racing through my mind. I had a fight with Brenda about wearing pants underneath my dress. It's the practical thing to do. I'm comfortable. I can cross my legs in public or during the meetings without worrying about keeping my skirt down. I warn you, someday all of the women in the United States will be doing the same thing and because I'm ahead of my time, because you can't foresee the event as I can, you clamp me in here. Wait, Doctor, just wait. So many of the things I wrote about to Eric Sevareid and James Reston are now coming true, but because I didn't use a copyright—because I didn't claim them as my own—I'm now paying the price of a lost identity. It's a wonder that they didn't clamp Einstein up for other people's failure to understand what he was saying."

"Eda, I'm going to put you on Mellaril. It will make you more comfortable."

"So that I can sit through the meetings?"

"You're very angry. Who are you angry at?"

"I'm angry at the forces of routine, stagnation, and obedience. All three spell instant impotence."

"I'll try this white pill. I want you to take it and tell me whether you change."

"Man, you may annihilate me physically, you can turn me into a vegetable, but you can't and won't destroy my mind. When you start to analyze how I think, then you're on the right track. Don't ask me how I feel. All that means is how hard I vomit or how fast I piss. If that's all you want to know, then forget about me, Eda Franchi, because then I die."

"Eda, take the pill."

"Gladly."

I exited quickly and marched back to my room. Brenda and the nurses were livid about my pants suit. "All right, you goddamn homos, I'll take off my pants."

Drew, who was in the hall, heard me and roared in approval, "You tell them, baby."

"I swear," I mumbled as I changed, "they're so goddamn concerned with how you look, how you eat, how you shower. I'm no more than an animal."

"It's not that, kid," Alix said, stopping me cold. "They have to start somewhere when you're so uptight. They have to start with the basics before you come back down to earth."

At two o'clock that afternoon, Alix came to tell me it was time for informals.

"What's informals?"

"We all gather around in a bedroom and look at each other. Drew usually trips out. We're supposed to discuss our problems."

Our group consisted of Herby, Inga, Drew, Alix, and Milly. The room was arranged with the chairs in a semicircle. Drew went straight to one of the beds. "I'm going to trip out on you kids. Just carry on." Drew had been doing this for weeks. He usually carried an Oriental philosophy book with him and started reading during the meetings. No one knew that Drew was slipping his medication under his tongue and later spitting it out in the john.

Milly turned to me as the meeting began. "Well, we have a new, restless member. Why don't we start by introducing ourselves."

Everyone repeated his name, except Herby who looked absolutely stoned. His forehead was sweating, his cheeks were red, and his eyes were popping out of his face. His lips were moving but he wasn't saying anything.

"Herby, say something. You've been here two weeks and you're as bad as Cathy." Cathy was another patient who had been in the hospital eight months and had spoken a grand total of five words. She looked worried and cried softly through most of the meetings.

I perked up. "Why doesn't Herby talk?"

"He was in a terrible car accident. He was Phi Beta Kappa before that."

"Most of you people seem too intelligent to be here," I said. "I really don't see what's wrong with you or why you're here."

"We all have our hang-ups," Milly answered.

"What are we supposed to discuss?"

"Anything we want to discuss—our problems, our feelings."

"But, Milly, if I say what I think, Drew will agree with me, and all the rest of you will think that my ideas are strange."

"Not necessarily strange. It's just that we don't think they're original."

"But I think they are and so does Drew."

"Eda, you just have to start participating. Right, Inga?"

"I can't hear you, young lady."

"You have to start participating, Inga. Do you hear me?"

"No, I don't hear you very loud."

"You have to try, Inga."

"I'm too old. And my husband won't change. He doesn't listen to me. He's from the old school, you know."

The hour was running out fast, and Herby hadn't said a thing. In fact, most of the people were just listening to Milly and me. I vented my anger toward the nurses about my pants suit and tried to explain to the rest of the group my feelings for knowing the future. I began to wonder if we were accomplishing anything.

As soon as the meeting was over, it was time for a different activity. At Easton Park, no matter how tired or drugged you were, you were expected to participate. The hospital ran on the principle of constant activity and discovery. Rest and relaxation were out the window. It was a painful process.

That afternoon we assembled in the hall to go to the gym. Most of us wore assorted combinations of clothes from our suitcase wardrobes. We looked so different from Vera, the activities leader from outside. Vera was slim, well dressed, fingernails polished—the perfect organizer. I went up, introduced myself, and shook hands. I had done this with most of the nurses on arrival, and they had found my handshaking out of order. Either no one shook hands or they hadn't been brought up to respect their elders.

We were ushered down the hall and across the street to the gym room. There another group of patients were playing volleyball. At first my feet felt loaded with lead, and anyway, I thought, I wasn't particularly interested in playing volleyball. But I shook off the stupor and, by the time our turn came, I was eager to play.

There were to be approximately twenty players on each side. Drew was a good player, and the captains argued about having him on their team. Even though I was enthusiastic and had a lot of confidence, I was the last one to be picked. I was on the same team as Drew.

Every time Drew scored, I would cry out or yell. No one else shared my enthusiasm. Finally Vera called me out of the game.

"Calm down, Eda. You're being too loud and the rest of the people can't concentrate on the game."

"But during a game you're supposed to be enthusiastic. Why isn't anybody enthusiastic?"

"Aren't you tired, Eda?"

"Hell no. I could go on like this forever."

"We only have fifteen minutes more and then a break until dinner at five."

"Gym certainly is short."

"Why don't you sit the next game out?"

"I don't want to sit the next game out, but I've got the hint that I'm too loud. I'll have a cigarette."

Maybe Easton Park wasn't the place for me. I went back to the ward to see Dr. Stein. I was ready to leave. Instead, I met Lucy in the kitchen. Lucy was always good to talk to.

"Hi, Lucy, it's Eda, the new girl."

"Well, I'll be. You're the friendliest cuss I ever saw."

"Want me to set the tables?"

"Sure. My, my, you set the tables and you clear the tables."

"I like to. I need something to do. I get desperate. And besides, you don't have to pay me."

"Eda, I hear that you also help with the beds in the morning and that you know Mimi and Belle."

"It's my job to be friendly and help others. That's why I'm here—to bring cheer."

"I sure don't know why you're here, but I'm glad to have the help."

I busied myself with setting the tables. I was also first in line so that I could load up on vegetables. Even though I was starving two hours later, I was determined not to put on weight. I would be like Gwen.

Tonight dinner looked delicious. I took my pick of all the lamb that was available and the two vegetables. I always ate a lot of vegetables.

I started to sit next to Alix and then moved to another seat. I felt that she and Milly were too protective. I still hadn't met everyone.

I chose a seat next to Peggy Sue. Peggy Sue was a plump, pretty girl, aged thirteen. She was also brilliant, but she found it hard to maintain any particular train of thought. Halfway through the conversation at dinner, Peggy Sue would get up and lie on the floor. No one appreciated this—especially not the nurses. Sometimes, Peggy Sue would be the only one, besides me, who would get up and walk out of the meetings. Peggy Sue offered no explanation. Peggy Sue was an epileptic.

"Would you like to see my butterflies?" she asked me.

"After dinner," Brenda interjected.

Peggy Sue, like myself, was followed around by Brenda or one of the other nurses. She had climbed up to some of the higher steps on the ladder, but then she would do something that bounced her right back down again. She was on a heavy dosage of tranquilizers, but it made no difference. Sometimes Peggy Sue would get so wild that the only way to control her was the wet-pack method. Wet packs were always the last resort. The patient was forcibly escorted by two nurses into a separate room and held in a tub of ice-cold water. Sometimes a patient would have to soak for two to three hours before he calmed down.

"What are your butterflies?" I asked.

"I make them out of tissue paper. It's the Japanese art of origami."

"Complicated?"

"Yes. I do all sorts of interesting things now that I'm out of school. I didn't find school very creative."

"Do you want to stay out of school?"

"I don't want to stay out of anything. But I want to participate on my terms."

"I would too, but nobody likes my terms. That's why we're all here. Because we don't like terms. How old did you say you were?"

"Thirteen."

"You sound a lot more intelligent than most thirteen-year-olds that I know."

"I am, but I don't belong. I cry a lot and sit in the middle of the floor and eat too much."

"You don't have to."

"I know."

At this point, dinner was almost over. I had become so interested in talking to Peggy Sue that my plate was still full. But I was made of gossamer wings and didn't have to eat to live. I was Eda. I was never going to die. I was never going to be bound to the banalities that concerned most people on the outside.

We had another meeting after dinner. I had already put in another bid to be raised to the next step. If I made it, I would leave Brenda for the sole custody of a patient.

Milly opened the meeting and called the roll. Alix and Jimmy had warned me beforehand to sit still and not to get upset. I might make it this time. I didn't, and the majority agreed that I wasn't ready. I was furious. I stood on the top of my chair and shouted at Milly, "What do you want? How long do I have to wait in this goddamn place before you listen to me? How do you expect me to try when you kill every effort? I've tried to be good and sit through your stupid meetings."

"You're just proving that you aren't ready, Eda—just by the way you're acting out now. I told you that if you cooled it, everything might be okay," Alix answered.

"Cool it?" I shouted. "You aren't willing to trust me and I'm not willing to trust you. I get along better with the cook and the cleaning help than I do with you. At home I was always more accepted by strangers than I was by my own. Mom thought too much of me, and Papa thought of me as nothing more than his baby daughter. I'm a lawyer, I'm an educated person, and I don't know why I have subjected myself to this shit. I'm leaving right now."

I stomped out of the room with Brenda at my heels.

"I'm leaving, Brenda."

"Eda, you can't."

"This is my second try, Brenda. First there was the pants suit. And now this. These people don't want to listen to me. No one wants to listen to me. I have to go to the bathroom and then I'm going to pack my bags and leave."

Brenda was beside me as I opened up my suitcase and started throwing stuff into it in a wild fashion. It was about nine o'clock at night. Suddenly Mom and Chris entered the room.

"I'm leaving, Mom. I'm going home to you and Chris. You're the only ones that cared in the first place."

"Eda, we can't help you anymore. You need this place and you need the people in it to help you."

Jimmy entered with his guitar hanging over his shoulder. He winked at Mom. "Hi, Mrs. Franchi. Gotta sweet-talk Eda into staying. She's a hot kid."

Mom smiled at Jimmy and then turned to me. But I didn't give her a chance to speak.

"Mom, I want to go home where I'm loved."

"Eda, you need professional help. Soon you'll be able to come home and you'll be better."

"I'm not sick. I'm just different. I've always been different. And now they're trying to make me like everyone else."

Chris asked: "Do you want to end up in another place like State, Eda?"

"No."

"Then be patient. I'll come to see you every night at seven o'clock. I'll refuse sea duty so that I can come to see you. Look forward to my visits if nothing else. But

I can't bring you home. There'll be no one to keep you company."

"I'll do like I did before. I had my ghost, my Chinese ring, my TV, my paintings, and my newscasters to keep me company."

Mom gave Chris the eye. Jimmy smiled and faded out into the hallway playing "House of the Rising Sun."

Mom said: "Eda, I think you had better stay."

"Stick it out a little while longer, Eda," Chris said. "Give the place a chance. You've only been here a week."

A week. Dr. Stein had told Mom and Chris that I would be in the hospital at least eight months. My case was serious. The chances of my leaving the place at all were slim.

After all the pleading, I calmed down. Brenda suggested that I call for Dr. Stein and arrange another visit. I did.

"Eda, I hear that you want to leave."

"Damn right I do."

"But your mother and Chris talked to you."

"It's fine to talk. They don't have to stay here."

"Why don't you just tell me that the tranquilizers aren't working?"

"No matter how stuffed I get with tranquilizers, I'm not going to change."

"Eda, are you going to stay?"

"Yes. I'm going to stay just to show you that I can take all the pills in the world, but I won't lose my enthusiasm. I think about things. I'm an intense person."

"Nothing's wrong with that as long as it can be properly channeled."

"Yeah, so that I can go out and do a half-assed job like the rest of the world. Nobody wants to change anything."

"You didn't like the world the way it was, so you sat back on your ass and commented from a rocking chair."

"That was the only way I knew how."

"You call that active? I can help you be more of a tiger than that. Will you stay and let me try?"

"Prove it. I'll give you one more week."

I kissed Chris and Mom good-bye, quickly unpacked my clothes, and everyone breathed a sigh of relief.

That night Dr. Stein increased my dosage of Mellaril. It had a relieving effect. It had its bad effects too. After my first dosage at midnight, I went to bed but not to sleep. At about two I wandered down the hall to ask the night nurse if I was on the blood-testing list.

"Eda, you still aren't asleep?"

"I keep thinking about the blood test. I get so psyched up that I can't sleep."

"Would you like another pill?"

"Yes."

"I'll have to ask the resident in charge. You're on a very stiff dosage as it is."

The only other one up was Herby. He wandered in, but still didn't say a word. His eyes were popping out of his head and his glasses were falling off his nose. The nurses had been pumping him full of Thorazine, but his dosage wasn't doing much for him either.

When the nurse returned, she went to the locked pill cabinet and gave me an extra pill. "You're not on the blood list for tomorrow, Eda," she said.

"Good. That's one more day that I don't have to worry."

"Most of the other patients don't."

"It takes me all night to think about taking it like a man the next day."

"Why don't you go back to bed?"

"Sleep is wasteful. People spend so many hours sleeping."

"They have to, Eda—for health reasons. I could take a nap myself right now."

"Well, back to bed. Here comes Herby. Why don't you open up your trap and say something, Herby? I talk too much and you say nothing."

I awoke at six the next morning and went in to see Lucy the cook and get my morning coffee. I took it into the main meeting room where I spent a good half hour with Belle discussing the cleaning situation at Easton Park. She gave me a wide, toothless smile: "You new here, ain't ya?"

"Yes, I like to get up early."

"You know Lucy too? She thinks you're the greatest help around."

"I'm glad somebody does. The nurses don't think so. You certainly cheer me up."

"We don't know much about medicine."

"I know. I'm happy when I talk to you people, but I'm sick when I talk to anyone else."

"Today's Saturday. Ain't you going out?"

"No. I'm not ready."

Lucy called and asked me to help with the tables. Setting the tables had become a daily ritual. I needed an active routine. Even though days were highly structured, I felt an additional need to work with my hands and with my body. I was still too exhilarated to sit down and really contemplate the seriousness of the therapy.

My most difficult moments were the meetings with the doctors and the patients. These lasted a minimum of two hours, depending on the number of patients attending and the topics discussed. My first task was to learn to sit still, never mind concentrate. After ten minutes, my thoughts would begin to wander and I would look for something else to do. I was very much like Peggy Sue who would sit in the meeting for a half hour and then get up to pace the floor. When the nurses asked her to sit down, she paid no attention. Sometimes she stayed out of the meetings altogether.

In addition to the general meeting, we had individual sessions with a doctor once or twice a week. And there were meetings where Dr. Solov, the chief of staff for "T" ward, would interview each patient to find out how he was progressing. Dr. Solov ran our ward and supervised the other doctors, all residents. He also personally handled the serious cases. He decided when some patients could no longer progress at Easton Park and he would have them transferred to the state hospital for long-term treatment.

We had other meetings too. On Saturdays we had long two-hour meetings to which parents were invited to join in the group therapy. At Easton Park, mental illness was considered a family problem. On this Saturday, Papa had flown in to visit me and also to attend the Saturday session. Mama and Chris were with him.

Herby's parents also came. They were both huge and doted on Herby. His father said: "Herby was a straight A student at Harvard, before he had that terrible accident. He was always such a good boy."

Alix's parents came. Her mother had red eyes. Alix didn't talk to either her mother or her father. Inga's husband arrived. He was a kind, distinguished-looking man of the old German school. He looked very much the wise professor, and did, in fact, teach at a nearby university.

The monitor called us in for the meeting. We broke into groups of four or five patients and their parents and four or five doctors. Then, in order to accommodate the large number of people, we had to clear out the bedrooms, line the beds up against the walls, and set up folding chairs. Herby, Alix, and Gwen, and their parents were in my group, as well as several doctors whom I had never seen before—including one I will never forget.

We started the meeting by introducing ourselves. A stony, awkward silence ensued. The parents and the patients were expected to talk, but no one said anything for five minutes. I felt uncomfortable and began: "Dr. Stein, I would like to hear from Herby. I've heard so much *about* Herby, but Herby hasn't said anything about himself."

Dr. Stein looked at me blankly. Herby's parents smiled. Herby's lips began to quiver, and he began to sweat. I was saying the wrong thing, but his silence bothered me more than creating an awkward situation. Herby's father started to explain about the auto accident. Silence followed.

I continued. "Alix, how are you feeling?"

"None of your business. I don't feel like talking."

"Okay, then I'll talk. I'm here against my will. I will stay one week and then I'm going home. I intend to help others and visit each ward to bring cheer. I am made of gossamer wings and I shall never die. Doctors here want to break your will and pump you full of pills. They don't listen and they don't believe in me. My parents say I'm sick, that I need help. Maybe I do, but a lot of people on the outside act nuttier than me. The people here don't believe in God, they believe in pills."

Dr. Katz, one of the other doctors, gave me one straight-eyed stare and then addressed the group. "Why doesn't someone cork her up?"

Stunned, I answered: "Then why don't you talk, stone face? When I say what I think, you tell me to shut up."

Dr. Katz repeated in a leaden voice, "When is somebody going to cork her up?"

I hated Dr. Katz for that. Alix was kinder. "Eda, you're rapping."

"Thanks, Alix," I said. "It's just the way I think and I don't want to die. I won't buy mediocrity."

Papa said nothing, but Chris offered a helping suggestion. "Eda, you're confused and could learn a lot from staying here."

"Yeah, by talking to Herby who says nothing and Alix who says it's none of your business. I've had enough. I'm leaving."

Dr. Katz stood in front of the door. "Mrs. Spaight, the meeting isn't over yet."

"I'm through with the meeting, Doctor."

"What's the matter? Can't stand to be told that you're wrong?"

"Don't worry. I'm not leaving the place. I'm just leaving the meeting. I have to get a breath of fresh air."

When I returned, the meeting was over. I had gone to the bathroom and then to the kitchen for a chat with Lucy. I met my parents and Chris in the hallway.

"A real jackass that Dr. Katz," I said.

"He doesn't know you, Eda. Are you going to stay?" Chris asked.

"Yes, dear. I have to prove a point."

Mom was solicitous. "Eda. We're going to leave you with Chris. We'll be down to visit you."

"Eda, remember that Mother and I love you," Papa added. "You have to stay here and take the cure."

I kissed Mom and Papa in the hall. Cathy and her parents were saying good-bye too. Cathy was wearing the new sweater her mother had bought her, and she was crying. "But I've been here eight months. You can't afford to keep me here. I'm no good." Both parents looked down at the floor and then left.

Herby's parents left with the promise to be back the next week. And in that week Herby progressed. His eyes came back into focus. He shed his usual hospital garb for a series of Brooks Brothers suits that had hung in his closet since his arrival. And Herby began to talk. He had a stuffed-mouth British accent, but he was talking nevertheless.

Physical testing was a new part of therapy. Brenda told me the next morning that I was scheduled for a brain wave test in some other part of the hospital. I was wary.

"Will it hurt, Brenda?"

"Not really. It won't hurt if you don't think about it."

"Will I feel an electric shock?"

"No. These tests are merely performed on an electric machine. It measures your brain waves."

I had to see Alix and find out what the test was all about. She was in her room strumming the guitar.

"Hey what, Eda?"

"Alix, have you ever had a brain wave test?"

"Yes, and I know what you're going to ask me. They don't hurt. Really. They're not as much fun as the personality tests. You aren't ready for them yet. But that brain test really doesn't hurt."

That afternoon I followed Brenda down the halls to the testing center. "Brenda, what will this test do for me?"

"Basically, it's a test for any brain damage."

I entered the room and sat in an overstuffed chair. Somebody in a lab coat told me to lean back and relax. I was scared, but it couldn't be any worse than taking a little Novocain at the dentist's office, I kept thinking. The lab man brought out a bunch of thin wires that looked like telephone circuitry with small tacks on the end. As I leaned back, he parted my hair and inserted thirty wires into my scalp. The pins pricked on insertion, but once they entered my scalp, the pain stopped. He went into another room and turned on the machine. "Now don't move your head, Mrs. Spaight. In five minutes it will all be over with."

As Brenda and I walked back, I breathed a sigh of relief. "I should have listened to you in the first place, Brenda. It didn't hurt. When do I take the personality tests? Alix says they're a blast."

"Not yet, Eda. You're not ready for them yet."

It was my third week in the hospital, and I was moved out of the big bedroom where all of the first arrivals slept into a smaller room with four roommates. Although I was still overly excited, I had calmed down considerably since I had arrived. My status was soon brought up at a meeting.

Milly asked me how I felt.

"Bad question, Milly. I always feel fine as long as things go my way."

"You've changed a lot, Eda. We think you're ready for the second step of the ladder."

I could hardly wait to tell Chris, who visited me every night as he had promised. It was a blessing to be able to see him away from the other patients. That night I was serious.

"Chris, you won't like me after my stay. I will change because I don't know what they're giving me here and because you've never really known me off drugs."

"Eda, I love you. I'll love you more off drugs than on them."

"But I might get fat."

"I never married you for looks, and you look a hell of a lot better than you did a few weeks ago. Your face has cleared up."

"My teeth have stopped bothering me too."

"Don't you want to live like a human being instead of going back to drugs?"

"I don't know. I don't like the way most people live. They survive; they don't enjoy. They just plod along. I'm going to be a great lawyer when I get out of here."

"Without pills."

"I can't promise. I ate so much for dinner that I could use one right now."

"But, Eda, the pep pills mixed you up. You would have been a great lawyer four years ago. You probably would have been a straight A law student. Even the doctors can't understand how you ever got through law school on thirty or forty pills a day. You wanted that degree so badly that you almost killed yourself."

"I wanted it more than anything else. I had to study hard, and pills were the only way I knew."

"Those pills never helped you through. They turned you into a bitchy, nervous little girl. It's just recently that I find you can be quiet. You can think for a change."

"You really want to travel that road six years back? I don't know what I was like six years ago. I can only take my parents' word, and they're biased."

"Eda, I want you well."

Soon I could hardly stay awake until bedtime. I was calming down rapidly and the rest of the patients noticed. I noticed too. Whenever a new patient was admitted, the difference between myself and him became clear.

When Blanche arrived, she looked like a witch and acted like a bitch. She arrived with thirty dresses—just a few things that she had brought from home. Her poor husband was burdened with carrying in all her magnificent belongings, and she shrilly told him to put everything in the closet. When they wouldn't fit, Blanche took out my clothes and shoved hers into my half of the closet.

Alix approached me in the hall. "Baby, have you got a ring-dinger of a roommate. They put her in your room because the big bedroom is full. She's already filled up her half of the closet and is starting on yours. Right now she's out in the hall hollering at Ted, her husband, because he didn't bring in everything. She thinks she doesn't belong here."

When I arrived on the scene, Blanche was out in the middle of the hall.

"Why did you bring me here, you jackass? I don't belong in a place like this. I wanted to go to a spa to relax. This place is for dope addicts and crazy people."

"Dear, the doctor said to bring you here," Ted answered.

The nurse interjected: "Blanche, please calm down."

"Calm down! Why in every spa that I've ever been in, I've always had a private room. I don't even have enough room in that goddamn closet for my clothes. I only brought a few things."

"Blanche, I'm afraid that your husband will have to take some of them back."

"But what am I going to wear?"

"Your husband can bring you more later on."

"My husband, goddamn him, has no right to leave me in this place with all these teen-age dope addicts. I want to go home. There's nothing wrong with me."

Ted spoke up at this point, when nobody thought he had the guts to say anything. "I'm leaving, dear. I hope you'll be in a better mood when I get back."

I went to Brenda immediately and told her the story of being booted out of half of the closet.

"Brenda, you know me. I'm willing to put up with a lot. But that bitch has to move a few of her things and put mine back in place."

"Eda, you've come a long way. Don't blow up now."

"I'm not blowing up. I'm just saying what ought to be done. She can't run the show just because she thinks this isn't the place for her."

I roomed with Blanche for three weeks until she was transferred to another room with a larger closet.

The next week three more patients were admitted. Two of them—Madge and Christie—came from another ward in Easton Park. Madge had just had an operation on her pancreas. The doctor warned that if she touched liquor again, it would be for the last time.

Christie was sixteen and had just had an abortion. Barbara, the third patient, had been admitted at the request of her parents and told no one why she was admitted.

In the meantime, Jimmy was discharged. He gave me a peck on the lips, strummed a hot chord on his guitar, and promised to come back and visit. He was off to Virginia.

Milly, Alix, Drew, Cathy, and I were now scheduled for the written personality and intelligence tests. They lasted about an hour and a half. We were excused from all the meetings that morning in order to take the tests.

Drew had already been through the series once. "They're great, Eda, some of the questions are a howl. They ask you whether you think you're being followed."

I sat down and was handed six sheets of paper. The first question read: "Today I feel (a) good, (b) very good, (c) fair, (d) not so good, (e) bad." I checked off box (a) and went on to the next question. The sheets were mimeographed so I knew that this series of tests had been made up by the hospital staff. All of the questions in the first six pages dealt with my feelings. There was one question that I couldn't answer. It read: "Do you feel that you're a worthwhile person? (a) Sometimes. (b) Never. (c) Most of the time." I crossed out all the answers and wrote in "I don't know. I'm Eda."

When our time was up, we were handed the basic intelligence tests. These were printed, and we were timed on each part. The problems dealt with simple arithmetic, reading comprehension, and vocabulary. Since there were no passing or failing grades, I enjoyed them. When we finished, our scores were recorded and we were scheduled for more difficult tests the following week.

Not everyone made it up each step of the ladder at Easton Park. We were all different. Even though we were on the same ward, it made no sense to try to classify our various situations as, for example, "nervous breakdown." We were there together because we didn't belong on the outside. Our highs were too high, our lows were desperate. It was discouraging to see a patient progress so far and then fall back into a condition where the only possible solution was to send him to State for long-term treatment. Sadly enough that's what happened to Herby.

Herby gradually opened up and started to talk. He changed into a new outfit twice a day. We became friends. We would sit out on the hospital porch. I would do my embroidery and Herby would pull out his English Lit book and read some poetry of John Donne or Keats or Shelley.

Herby moved up to the third step of the ladder. Then one day we had an informal. Drew, as usual, went to lie on the bed. I was sitting next to Alix, and Herby was sitting next to the dresser where I placed my soda. In the middle of our meeting, he started to change. His eyes were popping out of his head, and he started to sweat. Suddenly, he grabbed the soda bottle from the dresser and threw it on the floor where it shattered. The sound startled me.

"Herby, you didn't have to do that."

"Shut up. Bullshit."

"Herby, why did you do that?"

Herby walked out. He ran down the hall and started attacking one of the doctors with his fists. By the time I reached Brenda, two male attendants were holding him, and the doctor was giving him an injection of Thorazine.

After that, Herby gradually went downhill all the way. The only way to keep him at Easton Park was to keep him heavily tranquilized so that he wouldn't attack anyone. He went back into the hospital robe. He had a few lucid intervals, but always relapsed. He would be gay for a few days and then get violent. When I was finally discharged, Herby was docile and incoherent with his eyes popping out of his head and sweating profusely. He mumbled every now and then but made no sense. Later, he was sent to State.

Drew, too, was eventually transferred to the center for long-term treatment.

Many times when I talked to Dr. Stein at Easton Park, we talked about my family. Dr. Stein was convinced that I was afraid of Papa's wrath and that I was out to prove myself his equal. During one interview he questioned me.

"Eda, are your motives real? Do you do things because you want to, or because your family expects you to? Do you do things because your father did them and you think that you can do better?"

"I'm my father's child. My father was and still is a brilliant man. He's never failed."

"Eda, did you hate your father?"

"Why do you ask that?"

"Because you're capable of being as strong a person as he is. You can be a leader."

"I was a leader once. My parents said that I had many talents. Then when I started on pills, my interests narrowed. As I increased the dosage, I got so involved in busywork that I didn't have time for anything else. Whenever anyone came over to my apartment, including Chris, I was annoyed. I had too much schoolwork. He was a mercilous appendage."

"A what?"

"I made the words up. In other words, I was annoyed. He was an interference and that's why he fell in love with me. I wasn't interested, except on the weekends. We even drew up a treaty as to the times that we would be alone. Because he was human and I wasn't, he wanted to see me more often. That's when I really started popping pills. Every time that I hadn't planned a late night out or finished studying I would pop a pill. At home, when I didn't agree with Papa, I'd pop a pill and I'd be happy. It was a wonderful crutch. I don't know if I want to live without some kind of a crutch."

"Who told you to get good marks in school?"

"No one. I drove myself."

"Your father had nothing to do with it?"

"He was happy that I got them and bragged a lot about me. That's hardly a reason for saying that he pressured me into the grades."

"Did you ever flunk a course? What did it mean to you to flunk?"

"Utter, bleak failure."

"Eda, you've set such high standards for yourself that you'll never live up to them."

"I've always been a restless, exhaustive person—with or without pills. If someone gives me a job or I set out on a project, I go all the way. The thing has to be perfect when I'm finished. If I hate, nothing can change my mind. It works the other way too. If someone is my friend, I'll do anything for them."

"Does your husband know this?"

"He thinks he knows my potential if I would just forget about the ecstasy of drugs."

"What do you like about amphetamines?"

"I like the way they make me feel."

"You have an unrealistic picture of the way you acted when you were on drugs. You couldn't stick to one subject more than five minutes at a time—and now ten minutes at a time. What do you think your chances of becoming a lawyer are when you act this way?"

"Okay, okay, but I was active and enthusiastic about doing things. Every time I go off drugs, I lapse into a stupor, a long, long period of disinterest where I'm pulling myself through life with a twenty-pound weight around my neck. I don't want to go through life that way. So I pop a pill, pep up again, and have confidence in myself."

"But that's a drug-induced confidence. It's not the real confidence of a person who has accomplished something."

"Chris says that it will all be over when I pass the bar exam and get away from my parents."

"Eda, Chris may be taking the place of your father in shaping your own ideas about what you want to do."

"No. Chris isn't like my father. Chris encourages me to do my own thing. He just wants me to lay off drugs. He's kind and considerate of me in a way that my father never was. Chris is an angel, like my mother. I'm the one that's like Papa. I have a temper that's hard to control. I have a drive that's hard to alter once I've made up my mind. No, Doctor, Chris isn't like my father. It's just that he doesn't like doctors. He thinks my personality and background are so complex that you've underestimated me."

"Chris didn't think that you needed professional care?"

"No. He thought that I could withdraw from drugs at home on my own."

"Your parents talked you into coming here?"

"I was desperate. I couldn't burden Chris with the job of staying home with me night and day. But if he didn't stay, I'd go down to the local drugstore for a refill. I couldn't stand the shit that I would have to go through in order to recover a second time. But Chris hates the idea of my being a mental patient. I'm not sick; I'm his wife."

"But he isn't interfering with your recovery?"

"Not now. But it was a battle between Papa and Chris with me in the middle. My parents think I'm sick, Chris says it's easy to become well, and you treat me as an intelligent human being in trouble."

"Eda, do you really want to quit drugs?"

"Yes. I just made monitor and I have to review my duties for tomorrow. I'm uptight as a drum. If you had told me when I first came that I would take three months to make monitor, I would have told you to shove it—that I wasn't going to stay that long. I want out of this place, man, but on my own terms."

"Should I congratulate you?"

"That would be corny. I won't fit when I get on the outside. I'll be different in my own quiet, hellious way. I'll be misunderstood."

I had made monitor. The word had a golden ring in my ears. It was the highest rung of the ladder before a patient received the right to come and go from the hospital during the spare hours that were allowed him. After three months, I was on the threshold of departure from Easton Park.

Monitor was the main position of authority and responsibility. It meant that a patient was capable of managing his own affairs as well as telling others what to do in a nice way. That night when Chris came, I couldn't contain myself.

"Chris, I've made monitor."

"You'll be leaving soon then. Their original prediction about eight months in here was wrong. You only have one more step to go."

"Then I can go on the outside. I can sign out for overnights and go home on the weekends. Chris, it's been three months. I've forgotten what it's like to see a tree without the thick bars of the hospital windows. I've missed fresh air and stretching my legs in a fast, wirey pace. The tulips, peonies, and roses have come and gone without my living. I want to get out and taste it so badly."

"Are you ready?"

"No, I don't know. Let me take it at my own pace. Things will be a lot harder on the outside now. I have to be ready to face that."

"Eda, just think. We have a whole life ahead of us."

As monitor, I had to get up a half hour before the rest of the patients in order to remind those on the blood list about not eating. Then I had to attend the nurses' meeting at 6:30 A.M.

At the nurses' meeting, we listened while the night nurse went down the whole list of patients. As she read off the names, each of the supervising nurses looked at her notes from the day before and commented on the patient's behavior. On weekends, the monitor also took notes and at the Monday staff–patient meeting he would read his comments about each patient. I listened bleary-eyed to a few of the reports:

Herby: Markedly disorganized, mentally irrelevant, illogical; shows lack of concentration; appears inappropriate in his affects. When questioned about the accident or his admission to the hospital, smiles for no obvious reason . . . inadequate . . . continued medication of Thorazine with slight improvement.

Milly: Her parents visited yesterday. Mother had found ten dollars missing from purse. Milly noted to have been on Harly Street where dope pushers are frequent. Milly had outburst when questioned by mother regarding the missing money. Recommended that leave and trial visit status be removed.

Alix: Accompanied Milly and forgot to sign out and sign in. Recommended that all leave privileges be removed for those who forget to sign in or out.

Eda: Generally fairly congenial, showing a slight sense of humor at times, necessary to direct and encourage her. Still participates on a superficial basis with lack of involvement . . . elected to monitor yesterday . . .

After that meeting was over, I woke everyone up for the breakfast call. Then I had to round up a few volunteers to arrange the chairs for the three additional meetings we were going to have that day.

The first meeting was a big one. All patients who failed to sign in or out lost their leave status for a week. Dr. Solov's ruling was retroactive so it meant that Milly and Alix were grounded.

Milly spoke up: "You doctors think that you're gods. You give us less freedom than we can handle and then for a stupid administrative mistake you take away all our measly power."

"Miss Goldberg," Dr. Solov answered, "we didn't change the rules about signing in and out. We're merely enforcing them. Besides, you and I have other things that we must discuss at the next meeting with your parents."

We all knew that this meant the missing money from her mother's purse. The general suspicion was that Milly had stolen the money to go out on leave and buy drugs.

Drew also had forgotten to sign out. While on the outside and under the pretext of looking for a job, he had bought a new car. No one but Drew could explain this sudden whim, but it spelled doom for him. Like Milly and Alix, the staff felt that Drew couldn't be trusted. Perhaps the three didn't want to be trusted and were indirectly *asking* that controls be placed on them.

But Milly, in her high-hatted way, was convinced that the staff was against her. She was angry about being grounded and tried to persuade the rest of the patients that nothing was ever going to come out of our stay at the hospital.

The doctors continued with the meeting. By this time, I had learned to wait until I was called or my name was mentioned. I hadn't done this in six years. My usual habit was to listen first and then immediately tie up the experience with something that had happened to me. It gave me a chance to talk. Dr. Solov asked: "And who is monitor today?" I raised my hand. "And how do you like the job, Eda?"

"I have a hard time following everything on my list. It's three pages long."

"You have changed quite a bit in the last few weeks—almost as much as my red-headed friend Cathy."

Cathy had changed; she had opened up, whereas I had cooled off. She had been in the hospital nine months. For the first six to eight months, she stared at people, not answering their questions and bursting into tears at every meeting as soon as the doctors asked her how she felt.

In the meantime I had befriended Cathy. I talked to her even though she didn't talk to me. Most of the other patients had given her up as a lost cause. I wanted to get to know her. After many one-sided conversations, Cathy took my embroidery in her hands. She looked at it closely and murmured: "It's pretty." Then she looked at me with tears in her eyes. "I used to embroider. I used to do all those things."

"Really. What makes you think that you can't do them now?"

"I can't. I can't. I'm stupid."

"That's your business. I'd go nuts in this place if I had nothing to do."

"But, Eda, I'm no good."

"If that's what you want to believe, then go right ahead. Why don't you have your parents bring you something to do? I'll even help you."

"I don't know if they would do that. I think my parents are mad at me because I've been in here so long. I'm no good to anyone."

"No, not as long as you sit on your duff and think about it."

"I've been here so long that I don't think they have the money to pay for it."

"They'll worry about that. Come on. Have you ever played shuffleboard?"

"No. I don't know how."

"I'll show you."

That game was a real struggle. Cathy was full of misgivings about her competence. "Cathy, I'll play shuffleboard with you again tomorrow. And don't mope around the halls. Have your parents bring you some embroidery."

In the weeks that followed, Cathy and I became great friends. She visited with Chris and me on the evenings when her parents didn't come and she began to open up, although she was still a quiet, reserved person. She started to comb her hair and put on new clothes. Later on, she participated in many events at the hospital and became my companion when we took passes to go on the outside.

Cathy and I both changed for the better. However, as the days went by, Milly, for one, didn't fare so well. She had admitted taking her mother's money to buy drugs and she was grounded. She had been on heroin before, and now she began to trip out incessantly.

A blow-up with her mother triggered a violent reaction at her "Four Way." A "Four Way" was generally a meeting with the patient, the doctor, the social worker, and one of the parents of the patient.

Milly came out of the meeting shouting at her mother. "If all I did was take your money, you goddamn son of a bitch, then you ought to be happy."

Milly's mother gave her one fast swipe across the face. "Shut up, you little bastard. You never obeyed and you can stay here for all I care. I don't want a conniving little thief in my house."

Before Milly could really lay into her mother, she was in the forceful arms of the nurses to be carried off and soaked in wet packs. It was a Milly I'd never seen before. It was a Milly who had freaked out—not the officious little fat girl who used to conduct our meetings.

For several days after that, Milly stayed in her room. She had been busted back down in status to the third rung of the ladder so that she could be alone with no duties and fewer responsibilities. She spent a lot of time with Alix playing the guitar and with another curious visitor from the outside called Jehovah. He had once been a patient at the hospital and had been discharged A.M.A. (Against Medical Advice).

Jehovah had given up for the good life. He smoked pot and took the hard stuff. On certain days he would hang around the hospital lobby lying on the couches. Milly, Drew, Alix, and Jehovah were all part of the same crowd.

The only thing I liked about Jehovah was his looks. He had a build like an athlete, star azure blue eyes, and a crop of tousled, curly, sunbleached hair. Since summer was almost over, he sported a deep tan. He knew he was handsome and made the most of it. I didn't talk to him very much because I never talked to anyone that I was drawn to physically. The feeling was new and I was embarrassed.

Then one day Milly introduced me to Jehovah. He looked me up and down in a way that took off every piece of clothing I had on.

"What's your bag, babe?"

"Amphetamines. What's it to you?"

"Oh, the beautiful highs. And now you're trying to go straight. We could have a lot of fun staying on the highs. This place is for the birds."

"I've come too far to turn back."

"What do you do when you do your own thing?"

"I'm a lawyer."

Jehovah stretched out on the couch, put his hands under his chin, and smiled: "A sexy, strung-up lawyer. Honey, they'll ruin you in this place."

"Then why do you hang around here so much?"

"Because I've got friends that I've got to take care of."

"Alix, Milly, and Drew?"

"Yeah, we're attached. They don't really want this place either. But they've got nothing to go home for."

"I've got a husband to go home to."

"You're love-sick, chick. Wig out or you'll end up like the rest of the goody-goodies. Go to work; stay home;

have kids; and never really live. You'll groove in just like the rest of them—the silent, passive, mediocre majority—the yes-men—the cop-outs."

At this point I wanted to tell Jehovah that I was worth something, and that he was a schmuck. I wanted to tell him that for all his looks he wasn't worth shit. All he did was hang around the hospital being obnoxious. But my comments would have been pointless. Jehovah was an ass. Like Drew, he lived in his own world where he was king and he liked it that way.

Instead I looked at him sadly and said: "Man, I can't communicate. I wigged out for six years. How long have you been on the joy trip? When I wigged out, I did a hell of a better job than you. Tell me about your experience, snookie, when you've been a perpetual—when you've been on it so long that you've forgotten what you were like before you went off. Papa, when you've been big—not just a little short one-year run on the hard stuff. Come back and you'll know how beautiful you feel. You're big, daddy. Well, you're young and you're group stuff. I was private and that means discretion. Privacy means that you really enjoyed it and didn't need a whole gang to keep on going. Nice meeting you, but I've always been a loner. That's the way I go. I go big or not at all. And when I went, not even my husband knew. I had causes; I had the loves. You don't have the reason. That's why you can't take it without the group. Maybe I tripped out, but I loved it and your land, man, is no-man's-land. I'm going back to law. I'm different. I'm Eda. Ask about me in a few years. You'll never see me in this place again. I'm not an inner-outer. I'm a goer."

"You're still rapping, baby, rapping beautifully."

"Isn't that what you want to see? Isn't that what keeps your little group together? Isn't that why you need Alix, Milly, and Drew? So that you can all sit around and play the guitar together?"

"You're going to be a good girl, Eda. Sorry that you're on another wavelength. We could have made beauty."

I never talked to Jehovah after that encounter. When I saw him on the ward visiting and playing the guitar with

Alix and Milly, he'd smile and nod but we had no more communication.

Since I had been made monitor once, I took the job often. But I had now achieved the highest status—I could go out with a buddy patient during our free hours, and I was reluctant to be monitor on the ward all day.

As soon as we could schedule the time, Cathy and I signed out on pass. She was great company now. As we walked around downtown, we talked about future plans. Cathy wanted to go back to college. She was in her second year at a junior college.

"What actually happened to you, Cathy?"

"I don't know. I wasn't interested in anything anymore. I didn't want to see anyone and I stopped talking. That's when my parents took me to a doctor at school. He suggested they bring me here. I've been here the longest of any patient."

"So what? You're scheduled to be discharged soon."

"I know. But I hope that I never feel that way again."

"Could you control it?"

"No. It just happened. I remember you plugging away at me. Most of the patients made a joke out of me. They seemed to give up on me after the first six months. I was surprised that you would talk to me for so long when I just couldn't answer. It's so good to be on the outside again. Eda, we have to keep in touch after we get out. You have to come over to the house and spend a weekend. We can go sailing."

Chris was pleased with my new status because I would be going home soon. I had been in the hospital for five months. The doctors were pleased with my progress but reluctant to give me a departure date. I was first scheduled for a "Four Way"—with Chris, Dr. Stein, and the social worker, Miss Curtz.

Our "Four Way" was a flop. When I entered the room I was uncomfortable. No one bothered to initiate any conversation, so I started to talk. Chris said nothing. The doctor said nothing, and Miss Curtz said nothing. I felt like an ass, but I continued to rap. Chris looked at me in a strange way. Finally, I couldn't stand it.

"You know, I've been sitting here talking, and no one has said anything. Why are we here anyway?"

"We're here to discuss your problems," Miss Curtz said.

"But I've already discussed them at length."

"We thought that this meeting would help air any conflicts between you and your husband," Miss Curtz said.

"But there is no conflict between us. The only thing that we argue about is the method of treatment I'm receiving. Chris is convinced that I'm dependent on some kind of pills—any kind of pills—and would like to see me off them entirely."

"Eda is putting words into my mouth. I'm against indiscriminate pill-taking. Eda has to take a pill in order to feel good or bad. She's afraid of her own real feelings."

Miss Curtz interjected: "I hope that there are no sexual connotations involved."

I piped in: "Of course not. Now don't get me going on the sex bit. Somehow you single people think that it's all tied up with sex. What's a social worker so tied up in sex for anyway?"

Chris smiled. I was saying just exactly what he wanted me to say.

There was silence again. After ten minutes Dr. Stein said: "We have these meetings because we want to help the patient in relation to life on the outside. Chris and Eda, if you think that another meeting would be helpful, we will schedule one."

Chris answered: "I don't think that it would be productive. There's no conflict between Eda and myself as there may be between other couples. The conflict is between Eda and her parents. I know Eda better than most people. I've talked to you about her problems and explained them in depth."

We had no more "Four Ways," although I had been led to believe that they were a sign of ultimate departure from the hospital. "Four Ways" had proved most productive where there was a lack of communication either between child and parent or between husband and wife.

I began to press for an early release. Chris felt that I was well enough to have a trial visit home. But I wanted to take my time. I had been warned about the adjustments on the outside. Maybe I babied myself, but I felt that Chris was too impatient. Maybe he was just prejudiced against people telling me what to do. He knew that the last thing I needed was a father or father-figure to be afraid of.

Regardless of what Papa was really like, I had built an image. Papa Franchi was indestructible. He was the greatest man that I would ever know.

One evening, Chris told me, "You're very much like your father. If things don't go your way, you immediately blow up and almost go insane with rage."

"I never take things easily, Chris. I can't. I have a lot of ambition."

"But your temper spirals when you let it get out of control. Your brothers and sisters aren't that way."

"So? We've all been different from each other."

"You're all a very strange bunch. Your oldest sister doesn't even talk to Papa. Your younger sister had to elope in order to marry the man she wanted, and your brother doesn't want to fight in Vietnam, so he's living in Canada. You're the only one who ever listened to your papa and did just what he said."

"Except for drugs. And I took the pills to become a better lawyer. The doctor thinks that deep down I'm afraid of Papa. Maybe I am. I'm afraid that he may be mad at me. When we get together, we always say the same things. And yet, I depend on my family."

"Would you like to go and live in Syracuse when you leave here?"

"I wouldn't be able to see Dr. Stein. He says it's important to keep up my outpatient treatment for one or two years after I get out of here. If I go to Syracuse, I have to start all over again with someone who isn't familiar with my case. There's no guarantee either that I won't go back to my same old tricks. I don't want to go near Papa's office for a long time. I can swear up and down that drugs aren't worth it and that I'll eventually kill myself, but all I have to do is watch Papa eat three pieces of pie and go weigh himself and there I am, right on the scales, folding a bunch of prescriptions into my purse, living the same old way that I used to live. No, I want to go out on my own this time. Just you and me this time—without the family."

"Then we'll stay in Connecticut after I get out of the navy. But it will be a lot harder. We don't know anyone here."

"Chris, you haven't been sick. You haven't been an addict. I want to take it slow. I need to have all the help that I can get."

"I'll give you my all, Eda. When you're left to your own ways, you'll be a very strong person."

"Chris, I've never been on my own. That's what Dr. Stein told me. I've been independent, but I've never been out from under my family's wings."

After my talk with Chris, I had a pow-wow with Dr. Stein. I wanted out by December tenth. I would keep up treatment until that time. After that, I would see him twice a week and perhaps attend some group therapy sessions later on. He agreed that I would be ready for discharge in approximately a month.

"Eda, we wanted you to tell us. You have to learn to assert yourself rather than waiting for everyone else to tell you what to do."

"But Doctor, you and Chris are telling me what to do right now. It's because of you that I'm staying here in Connecticut. Chris wants to move back to Syracuse."

"We encounter this with so many patients. I'm trying to have you know yourself better so that later on doctors will be superfluous."

"I'm not sure I understand. When I first came here, the nurses were giving me orders. Even as a monitor I had a schedule of duties that kept me in line with hospital rules."

"When you get on the outside the hardest thing you'll face is the lack of rules—the total lack of structure. You need to establish a pattern—a routine."

"But you tell me to take my medication and Chris tells me to cut down. So I've tried to cut down."

"Eda, you're starting to get nervous and skip subjects. If you're going home soon on trial visit, then I'll have a talk with Chris about your medication."

"I don't know if I'm quoting him correctly. He says that I always misquote him and exaggerate."

"There's a conflict between you and your husband."

"Only because I'm making him into another Papa."

"What do you mean?"

"Because I'm always asking him what to do. He straightens out my thoughts for me the same way that you do."

"Why don't you make a trial visit home this weekend just to see how things work out?"

"I'll try. Chris will be ecstatic. We've waited so long. I've even forgotten what home looks, smells, and feels like. Maybe Chris's changed my exotic garden."

I signed out for a weekend at home. Chris was pleased and planned to be around all the time that I was there. Basically, I was afraid. How was I going to face all of the navy people who knew about my situation? I didn't want them offering pity or help. I only wanted Chris's guidance.

That night at home we talked about future plans. On final discharge from the hospital, I'd get a job. That would fulfill Dr. Stein's warning that I needed structure. I wasn't ready for a law job since my powers of concentration were minimal. Yet, I had no idea of anything else. We'd be moving to a new town soon, since Chris was about to be discharged from the navy.

Chris's discharge was a hardship discharge—hardship because of me. When all of the officers received the news that their tour of duty had been extended another year, Chris became desperate. He didn't want to leave me for a six-month trip at sea and accordingly put in for a hardship discharge. Chris liked to be with me and wanted to be with me always. And he was vital to me, especially after his discharge.

Chris had ambition. A graduate of the University of Wisconsin School of Chemical Engineering, he'd spent four years in the Navy Nuclear Submarine Corps and had picked up a lot of training on running nuclear reactors. To him the future was limitless. He was going to go out and get a job that would earn him the presidency of a big corporation. I was going to be a big-time lawyer and make lots of money. We were young and we were determined. We thought that was all it would take.

My initial plan as laid out with Dr. Stein was to get a simple job—to occupy my time until Chris got out of the navy. Chris volunteered to get me a job with Navy Relief. It was part-time and volunteer, but at least I'd be close to him. The next step of the plan was more difficult. I would get a paying job, part-time and simple. Finally, I would get a job as a law clerk and study for the bar exam in the meantime. Ultimately, I would become a full-fledged lawyer and set up my own practice.

Chris's plan was to stay in the navy until discharge and then move nearer the hospital. From there he would decide on employment. He was equipped for the decisions that were made at the time. I wasn't. In the years that followed, I longed for the supporting role of my parents but realized that the whole thing was wrong. I was in the big leagues now. I could no longer turn to my parents and I had the responsibility of marriage to contend with. But as yet I was only home on trial visit. I had three more weeks in the hospital before the final plan would take effect.

I had misgivings about being discharged. Alone in the apartment I'd face lack of a routine. I couldn't turn to my old follies of polishing the furniture, painting on windows, flying kites, and writing to the newscasters. I had stopped watching television on Dr. Stein's advice. Every time one of the patients would turn on the news, there I was, Eda all over again, with my ideas influencing the world.

While I counted the hours until the Friday afternoon trial visit home, I again began to notice the contrast between myself and the newer patients. It seemed that we came from different worlds. I saw various phases of my old self in each personality that arrived at Easton Park.

At the big meetings I was usually quiet, but others

weren't. Milly, Alix, and Drew were still belligerent, and their leave and trial visit rights hadn't been reinstated. At one meeting, the doctor turned to me and asked me directly: "Mrs. Spaight, you're scheduled for discharge, but don't you still have disagreements with the staff?"

"You mean when you took my bed away from me?"

"It had bars on both sides. We thought you didn't need bars anymore."

"I became attached to that bed—bars or no bars, you could have told me beforehand."

"We didn't think that you'd get upset and cry."

"I got over it, didn't I?"

"That's the only reason that we didn't cancel your trial visit home this weekend. We don't mind if you cry. We only ask that you get over it. Do you still feel persecuted about it? Are you comfortable in the new bed?"

"No, but I'm not staying here much longer."

"Try not to let little things upset you so much. Adjustments here are ten times easier than those that you'll have to make by yourself on the outside."

Chris came and took me home that weekend. We went to the officers' club and talked about getting the job at Navy Relief. I made the mistake of relying on Chris to go everywhere with me, show me how to do everything, and provide entertainment when I was bored. I wasn't capable of forming my own opinions, nor did I have any distinct identity other than being his wife. I was a very timid creature, self-conscious and blah, when I wasn't talking about having had a "nervous breakdown."

Although I became intensely bored with the hospital routine, Easton Park was always trying new ways of making the patients discover themselves. On return from trial visit that weekend I was informed that we were supposed to attend a play. I nudged Alix. "Who's coming here to perform for us?"

"Nobody, we're the actors and the actresses. Let's go. We're supposed to be in the meeting room right now."

The "psychodrama" that was using our patient talent

was organized by a group of trained psychologists. One of the three men explained that they were going to call on the patients and ask them to act out certain situations.

"Another yo-yo device," Alix whispered to me.

The speaker called on Herby. He was in a talkative mood and stood up to introduce himself.

"Where are you from, Herby?"

"Pennsylvania and then Harvard."

"Did you finish college?"

"Yes. I was Phi Beta Kappa."

"Herby, I want you to talk to a high school dropout. I want you to convince him of the value of returning to school to get an education. I will call on members of the audience to evaluate your speech."

When Herby was finished, the speaker called on Alix and Drew. "Why are you two here?"

"Because Drew took LSD and I used to shoot up heroin in California," Alix replied.

"Come up here and sit down. I want you to remember and give us a picture of what it was like to run out of drugs. I want you to show us your physical and mental reactions."

When Alix and Drew finished, the speaker turned to me. "Eda, that's your name? Come up front. I want you to describe a tree. The tree shows the alternatives that you now face in your life. Tell me how many branches it has and what you see for yourself in the future."

"I see three branches on the tree . . . The first one is sad. It shows me going back on pep pills. If I follow that branch, this place will become my permanent home. I will lose Chris, my husband, because I'll eventually be declared incompetent, a chronic drug addict. I'll be transferred to the center for long-term treatment or to a state hospital. I will live and die with my original diagnosis scratched on some doctor's notepad: schizophrenic reaction, paranoid type, severe, manifested by visual and auditory hallucinations, ideas of reference, delusional thinking, drug-induced, incompetent. The second branch means that I get out of here and stay off drugs. Since I'm a lawyer, I become a member of the bar and practice my profession. I eventually set up an office, work hard, and become successful. The third branch is another workable alternative. Since I speak four languages, I either get a legal job or one that takes advantage of my language ability. It would be more of a nine-to-five type job that would leave me time to have hobbies other than law."

The speaker called on Alix. "Alix, do you think that Eda will follow the first road that she outlined?"

"No, Eda will go straight. We want Eda to go straight. She's changed a lot in these past few months."

The speaker pursued the point. "Alix, will you go straight?"

"Why should I? Eda has a wingding husband who's somebody to live for. My mother had me out of wedlock. I have nobody that I want to go home to. I hate my mother. She loves me but I can do without her. I've got to find something else to live for."

The speaker turned to Drew. "Drew, will you go straight?"

"I don't know. I'm still tripping out. I don't take the stuff anymore but I still trip out. Eda used to believe in Lao-tzu but she doesn't anymore. I'm afraid Eda's no longer with us—Alix, me, and Milly. We're still hung up on the good life. Eda's leaving us next week."

Part Three

The hospital doors closed softly behind me as I stood, suitcase in hand, waiting for the car. Chris had already made arrangements for my job interview, but my lack of confidence was beginning to show.

"Do you think I can handle it, Chris?"

"It's a start, Eda."

"I don't know if I can drive anymore."

"You didn't forget. Don't worry; I'll be working at the base now, so I'll take you down there next week. Mr. Stone will interview you. He doesn't know about your past. He knows that you're a lawyer. Remember that and stop thinking of yourself as a patient on 'T' Ward at Easton Park."

"But do you really think that I'll be able to handle the job?"

"It's only for half a day. I can take you in the morning and meet you for lunch at the officers' club."

"Sounds good. You know how tired I get in the afternoon."

"But you don't have to sleep. You didn't sleep in the hospital."

"They wouldn't let me."

"Take fewer of those damn pills. You still think that the medication's helping you. Eda, you've done it on your own. How do you know that you couldn't have recovered without tranquilizers?"

"Dr. Stein told me so. Have you forgotten so quickly what a wild nut I was when I went into Easton Park? This time, I'm doing exactly what the doctor says."

Before my job interview, I stayed home alone in the apartment. I tried to set up a routine, but it worked only to a slight degree. After Chris left, the question faced me point blank: What do I do now—and later—and after that? I'd go back to bed and swear that I'd do the shopping later. When Chris came home for lunch, he'd ask me what I did.

"I went back to bed."

"When you start the job, you won't be able to go back to bed."

"Okay. But right now, I've nothing to do. TV doesn't interest me anymore. I can't read and I'm not very good at cleaning the house."

"Why don't you visit with the neighbors?"

"Because I can't stop talking about the nervous breakdown. I think I'll take a nap this afternoon."

"Eda, you have to face life, and life isn't sleeping thirteen hours a day. Now that you're off the pep pills you worry about not getting enough sleep."

"Chris, if someone could dream up a pep pill that didn't have such bad side effects, I'd take it. I felt awake then. I was alive and interested in everything. Now I don't give a damn. Sleep is nice."

"It's productive for you—a way to pass the time. Don't talk like that, Eda. You're still pill-crazy. By God, you'd rather take a pill than figure things out on your own."

"I'm taking the right pills now and the right dosage."

"See that it stays that way for a change. By the way, Mr. Stone will see you the day after tomorrow. You can ride in with me in the morning and write letters before you go to work."

"That's a good idea. Writing letters will keep me busy and you'll be right there."

"Well, I'm going back to the base. Why don't you start a marathon cleaning of the house before you go for the interview?"

I started cleaning, but it was basically a matter of pacing myself. I'd wash one set of dishes, put them away, and say to myself: What next, Eda? I went to the supermarket. I wandered up and down the aisles looking at all the new products. Did I want to cook? No. That involved eating. I might cook something that I liked and eat too much and get fat. Then I'd end up looking like Aunt Gabriella. I walked out of the supermarket empty-handed.

I went to visit Paula, my next-door neighbor.

"How've you been, Eda? I didn't want to stop by because I didn't know what you were doing. I'm getting the house ready for the baby that's due in December. See how big I'm getting?"

We chatted the whole afternoon about the coming baby and all of Paula's plans. I felt glad to have some company. However, in the back of my mind and all the time that I was talking to Paula, the idea haunted me: Was I really ready for discharge? It had to come to the surface.

"Paula, do I seem normal? Do I appear different to you now than I did then?"

"You're much more relaxed than when I last saw you."

"I feel so lost and so left out. Chris lined up a job interview for me tomorrow and I don't have the confidence to sharpen a pencil, let alone act like a lawyer."

"You never worried as much as you do now. Other than that, you seem fine to me. Why don't you come shopping with me tomorrow?"

I didn't want to bother Paula, but I failed to realize that housewives are more adjustable in the time that they have to spare. I wandered around after my visit, counting the hours until Chris arrived. I had some frozen cherry kuchen in the refrig, so I pulled it out and followed the easy recipe on the back. When he came home, it was ready. Chris's encouraging words made me wonder about Dr. Stein's previous analysis: "Eda, don't do things to please your papa all over again."

I went in with Chris the next day for my appointment with Mr. Stone. He smiled a lot and treated me with respect.

It took a week to establish a very pleasant routine that would last until Chris got out of the navy. I rode in with him, spent the morning chatting with the wives at Navy Relief, met him for lunch at the officers' club, went home and took a nap. Once a week in the evening I was scheduled for group therapy. I wasn't hot on the idea, but Dr.

Stein thought it would help. I didn't want the help of others. I wanted to help myself.

In the meantime, I received a letter from Cathy. She'd been released and invited Chris and me down for an afternoon at her parents' home in Salem. As I read the rest of the letter aloud to Chris, I checked the signature.

"Chris, that doesn't sound like the Cathy that I knew. She's talking about having a blast dating and sleeping with two or three boys a night. Maybe I'm reading too much into the letter."

"How old is Cathy?"

"About nineteen. And her parents are so nice—so well bred. Her mother went to Wellesley or Sweet Briar."

"Don't prejudge. Wait until we go down there in two weeks."

Two weeks later we were driving up to the spacious home of Cathy's parents. Although her parents must have paid a fantastic hospital bill—$90 a day for ten months, not including doctor fees and medication—it didn't seem to affect their financial status. The grounds were well kept and the entrance smelled of fresh paint.

Cathy met me with a big smile. She wore lipstick, had her hair done, and was dressed in a light blue sweater set. We chatted with her parents, who were also concerned about post-hospital treatment. Finally Chris took over, and Cathy and I adjourned to the bedroom to talk about old times.

As soon as the door closed, she started to talk about the letter. "You see, Eda, my parents don't know that when I say that I'm going to stay overnight at Lucy's, I really go and spend the night with John and Larry. It's a blast. I've been going to their place almost every weekend. You won't tell. You're part of the secret now—the secret conspiracy."

"Have you told your doctor about this?"

"No. He wouldn't understand. Want to see my thing?"

Cathy opened the drawer and pulled out a foam injector for birth control. I spent an hour listening to her sexual exploits and then resolved to cut our ties of friendship. When I received more letters, Chris told me to throw them away and forget about Cathy.

"Eda, that's probably why she went into the hospital in the first place, although she never told you."

While Chris interviewed for jobs, I continued my work at Navy Relief. My co-workers soon learned about my past. I needed some excuse for not being a lawyer. I kept repeating the same questions that I had asked Paula: "Do I seem normal to you? I just got out of the hospital for a nervous breakdown. But please don't tell Mr. Stone."

I also developed a habit of drinking coffee. When there was nothing else to do, I'd pour another cup. By the time I joined Chris for lunch at the officers' club, I had a real coffee stomach. Chris usually had a beer and bought me one too.

"One can't hurt you, Eda. You'll relax. I'd rather see you have one beer than take one of these pills."

"But I'm supposed to take the pills. I never asked the doctor about liquor."

"Have a beer and forget about the pill."

"I'd like a beer. But I can't make a habit of this."

Chris had nothing against alcohol, but he forgot how capable I was of overdoing things. It didn't show then.

Six months later, we made the big move to a new town, and a new apartment. Step two of the plan was in operation. I was out looking for a paying job. I interviewed all over the place, only to find that a lawyer is qualified for law alone. I had no idea of what I wanted to do and felt less qualified each time I came home from an interview. Most of the jobs advertised in the paper were typical female openings—clerks, typists, shirt pressers, waitresses, etc. Every interview was disappointing: "I see that you're a lawyer. Why do you want this job? Do you know how to type? Can you take steno?"

Finally, I interviewed at Sears. The job was for a table busser. I explained the whole situation to the personnel manager.

"But, Mrs. Spaight. You're a lawyer. You must have brains."

"I'm not sure that we're going to stay in Connecticut but I'd like to work in the meantime. You have to be a member of the bar to get anything else," I explained.

"You seem overqualified for the position. I'll think about it and let you know."

Job-hunting was tiresome. As I sipped my cocktail before dinner, I told Chris that I wanted a job—any job—and that I was willing to try. Chris had decided to stay with a small metal-plating company which was a five-minute drive from home. He wanted to stay close by and felt the need to keep an eye on me until I got a job.

Finally, I got the job at Sears and was introduced to the kitchen help. Every day that I came home from work, I was exhausted.

"Better let up on those pills, kid."

"Not until the doctor tells me, Chris."

"You don't need them now. You're working. Have a drink before dinner if you need to relax and then skip the pill."

Even though I was out of the hospital and working, adjustment to a normal, established routine was a slow process. I wasn't interested in getting up because I faced the gnawing problem of keeping myself busy. I didn't start work until nine o'clock. I would get up at six, make breakfast, take a pill, and go back to bed. Pretty soon, the excess sleeping began to bug me. Dr. Stein then had me keep a tally of the hours that I slept.

"Eda, the pills don't make you sleepy. You've merely gotten in the habit of going to sleep every time you're alone."

"I can't get interested and I'm afraid of being too tired to do a good job at work."

"You're too worried about your physical well-being. Stop thinking about what you're doing and just do it."

"But you taught me to think about myself."

"You and Chris overdo it."

"We talk about our plans. I've come a long way now. I'm in step two of the plans."

"Chris is telling you what to do."

"He's not telling me. I'm asking him. I'm not capable of making such big decisions."

"Keep the sleeping chart. You have to realize that one reason that you come to me is so that Chris doesn't have to assume the professional responsibility for your progress."

"But he's interested. You only see me for an hour."

"So be it. I'll expect you at the group therapy meeting next week."

Our first group therapy session included four patients, besides myself. Drew was still in the hospital, bobbing between long-term treatment and discharge. Madge had husband problems, a child that she didn't want, and an alcohol habit that had put her in the hospital in the first place. Bob was a middle-aged, successful executive who couldn't decide whether to leave his wife and family for another woman or merely switch jobs for something more challenging. He didn't want to throw fifteen years of a forced marriage down the drain and was unhappy with the routine of a middle management position. Myron was a high school principal who was homosexually attracted to his son—a drug addict.

Myron began, "I want to be friends with everyone and hope to gain some insight and uplift from our sessions."

"What are you trying to say, Myron?" Madge asked.

"I want to be your friend and I need your help."

I spoke up: "How can you want to be friends when you don't even know us? That comes on a little strong."

"Well, we're all here for a civilized purpose. By coming here, I hope to work through some of my inner conflicts."

"What's wrong with you?"

"It's so touchy that I'm really not prepared to commit myself to anything definite at the moment. Say that I'm confused."

Dr. Stein interrupted. "Eda, you're coming on a bit frank. None of the other patients have done any talking."

"All right. I'll shut up. But so far, I'm not getting much out of this meeting."

"Don't cross-examine, Eda."

I said to myself, Shit. They're all crazy. Drew is still

tripping out and undecided. Bob will take off through his girl friend's skivvies and then cry to us that he ought to stay married for the sake of the kids. Madge is putting on a good front, but she may get drunk this weekend. There's something about Myron I can't stand.

When I came out of the session, Chris was curious. "Eda, what are they going to do for you?"

"I don't know. This was only my first session."

"What could you possibly have in common with those people?"

"I shared a hospital with them once."

Eight months of work at Sears had passed, and Chris started to push the legal job. So, in my spare time, I started to look for something in law. I hounded the local Legal Aid Society and promised to take the bar exam the next time it was offered. I finally got the job, gave Sears notice, and brought the good news home to Chris.

He was thrilled. We analyzed each other over a drink that night. Chris talked me into having a Manhattan and skipping the evening dosage of tranquilizers.

"Eda, I'm so proud of you. Just think. You're on your way to becoming a lawyer and you did it on your own."

"With Dr. Stein's help."

"You did it on your own," he repeated.

The law office of the Legal Aid Society was staffed with second- and third-year law students who worked on a part-time basis. My boss, Mr. Green, wanted me to specialize in bankruptcy, since that was my strong point in law school. They had only two full-time lawyers and I was to be the third—as soon as I passed the bar.

Clients were standing in the waiting room, but instead of meeting with them, I was given a booklet explaining the organization. It was the first thing that I was supposed to read and digest since I had entered the hospital. I went to my cubicle poring over the thing, trying to memorize rather than read.

At one o'clock, Milt, one of the students, told me that

I was free to get some lunch. I had no idea where to go, and I was used to having lunch at around four in the afternoon. I wasted an hour eating two scoops of cottage cheese and went back to the office. On the way home that night I bought a Dubonnet. I needed a drink. No nap. No interviews.

When Chris came home, I poured two drinks and we sat down.

"How was it, counselor?"

"They gave me a booklet to read. I'm just exhausted."

"Take it easy on that drink. This stuff hits you kind of fast."

"The bar exam is in February. Tomorrow they may start me interviewing the clients and give me some cases to work on. Today was an introduction."

"Eda, the whole week will be an introduction. As the job gets harder, it takes longer to learn."

"It's so different from Sears where I was punching a time card. I want to be watched and told and shown. I really don't know what I'm doing."

"You're a professional. You don't punch time cards."

But even after I started interviewing the clients, writing up complaints, and completing briefs, I felt as though I never really knew the work. Either the interest was lacking or the ambition was gone—evaporated. I didn't bother to explain my frustrations at the group therapy sessions. I didn't want anyone's help. I didn't want to go to any more meetings, but I did.

Myron was still a homo, and his son had come home from the hospital and torn apart every painting in Myron's art collection with a pocket knife.

"Why didn't you go after him with a belt? That's what my father would have done, sure as hell."

"Eda, he really didn't mean it. I love him so, I just couldn't raise a hand to him. The boy's sick."

"That's why he's sick, Myron. Beat the hell out of him like a normal kid and maybe he'll act normal."

"I really can't blame him. It's his own way of getting back at me because he knows my feelings. I want to make love to him."

"That son-of-a-bitch brat is testing you with all he can get away with."

"But I love him, just as I love all of you."

"Yick!"

"I want to be friends and nobody wants me."

"You're slimy, Myron, that's why. Chin up and act like a man. I don't care how queer you are. Lots of queers act like men."

"Then you reject me too."

"I'm telling you what to do and you burst into tears. You stay the same and aren't willing to take a new step."

"Eda, we all want to try. We all want to help each other."

"Bull. Have any of you changed your position since we started these sessions? No. We find out that Bob had to get married. Eda repeats her same story about former drug addiction and her latest progress at the office. Madge admits that she had an affair while she was married, and Drew is still in the hospital tripping out. Damn it, I'm not coming any more."

As usual, Dr. Stein was on my tail to cool it. "Eda, you're upset."

"You're damn right, Doctor, and it's about time. What's wrong with being fed up? You don't want to hear what I've got to say. So good-bye."

At our private session Dr. Stein told me to hang on until June when he would complete his residency requirements and move out of state. He would make arrangements for me to see another doctor.

That night, I told Chris about Dr. Stein leaving.

"You stayed here for him, but he ain't staying here for you. Do you need him at the cost of twenty-five bucks a session?"

Chris had a way of always worrying about money, even though I had some cash and some very lucrative stocks.

"I don't know. I hate to go against his advice. I want to be sure that I'm well before I quit. And stop worrying about the goddamn money. I'm sick of hearing about money."

"How well is well and what is well? We're all a little

nuts. Just think about it, Eda. You made a life decision to stay in Connecticut for him. Now he's up and off. If you didn't pay his bill, he really wouldn't care about you at all. You only go to get the pills anyway—those magic pills that keep you calm."

"I've cut down on the pills, Chris. I've had a few drinks at night instead. If it weren't for the money, I'm sure that you wouldn't object to the treatment. I'm so sick of hearing about how much he charges me. Pills were more expensive. They cost me six years of my life."

"He and any kind of pills are a crutch."

"I want to continue seeing someone until the bar exam."

"Stay on the pills until the bar exam? It may hurt your chances of passing."

"Let the doctor tell me, will you?"

"When you pass the bar, you'll have some confidence. But Stein's not going to help you with the exam."

We cut the discussion short. I decided to continue with Dr. McGuire, who had been recommended by Dr. Stein before he moved out of state. I made an appointment that next week and left work early.

I was upset. I was nervous and jumpy. I had to like Dr. McGuire before I would gain any confidence in him. I'd been off tranquilizers for a week. Dr. McGuire opened the door. His office was plush and new—nothing like the clinic where I had seen Dr. Stein.

Dr. McGuire sat down and looked at me. I looked at him. Five minutes passed. Finally, he looked at my appointment card. "Mrs. Spaight?"

"Yes, Doctor, I have a lot of problems." I then started out in a long monologue about my work and lack of confidence. "Dr. Stein has given you all the details about my hospitalization at Easton Park, hasn't he?"

"He outlined your case roughly, yes. How do you feel now?"

"Miserable. I've been off my medication for a week and I don't sleep at night. I just started a new job and I'm up in the air about that. My husband didn't want me to start with you in the first place."

After ten minutes, my monologue ran out. I wasn't used

to talking and not getting advice. I didn't appreciate the five minutes of silence that followed. I wanted help.

"Why don't you say something, Doctor?"

"I want you to talk, Mrs. Spaight."

"But I don't want to talk all the time. I just got over that. What do you want me to talk about?"

"Your problems."

"I've already explained my problems."

"From what you've told me, I think that you need to go back on your medication and that you need in-depth analysis. You have deep-rooted problems."

"What's in-depth analysis?"

"Since you've said that money is no concern, I would like to see you at least three times a week."

"Three times a week! But I was only seeing Dr. Stein once a week or once every other week. He thought that I was progressing. Now you tell me three times a week. Look, with the help of the medication, I think I could cut it down to once a week."

"You're upset."

"Yes! My husband will never agree to my coming three times a week."

"Think it over. In the meantime, I'll write you a prescription. I think that you need the medication."

I stomped down the stairs and banged my thumb in the door. I was livid. I added up the figures in my head: $40 a session, three times a week, a total of $120 a week. I couldn't afford it. How could I have retrogressed to the point that I needed to go three times a week? I would bargain; once a week or not at all.

I bought a bottle of Seagram's Seven on the way home. When Chris entered, I had a Manhattan waiting for him. I took a big gulp of my own drink and broke the news.

"Eda, he said that he wanted to see you three times a week. That's $120 a week! We flat out can't afford that kind of money. Did you tell him how much money you had?"

"Yes, but when I told him that I didn't have much income, he suggested that I sell some of my IBM."

"He's telling you how to manage your finances to pay

him. Eda, don't be so stupid. We're all human. We're all greedy. When you told him you had money I'm sure that the cash register was clicking away. Judgment: three times a week. She can well afford it."

"Damnit, Chris, I'm back where I started."

"Listen to me, Eda."

"I agree with you. How about telling him once a week or not at all?"

"You mean you trust him after this?"

"Chris, I have to see somebody."

"Then find Stein; tell him that you don't like this guy and have him recommend someone else."

"I don't know where Stein is. I think he's left the state. Look. Let me try this new doctor once more. You can even meet him."

"I certainly will."

I soon began to lose interest in my work. I arrived later each day. I was falling behind with my research and I'd spend hours chatting with clients. The office operated on a shaky budget, so that every time Mr. Green called me into his office, I thought I was going to be fired. I never explained this fear to Chris.

Chris was preparing to go out on the road selling chemicals. His year of working at the plant was up. The move to New Jersey as Chris's settling territory had been announced after much delay. I was faced with the choice of taking the Connecticut bar or putting the whole thing off until we moved. I couldn't see taking the exam in a state where I would never practice.

Chris's attitude was different.

"Eda, you don't know for sure that we're moving, so why don't you take this exam? You're afraid of flunking? Flunk. It won't be the end of the world."

"I'm not afraid. I just can't see the wasted effort when we aren't going to stay here. I've even stopped going to the doctor."

"McGuire's nuts. He's the nuttiest doctor I've ever met. Didn't even say hello to me."

"I have no one else to go to. Maybe I should see someone when we move to New Jersey."

"That's just what your parents would advise. When are you going to stop relying on doctors and rely on yourself?"

"I need a professional."

"That's your father's opinion. Everything can be solved by sending you to a doctor. Eda, I've lived with you through all this and I'll be happy to see the day when you're off doctors, pills, and recommendations from everybody. It all boils down to a lack of confidence in your own ability to succeed."

"God help me, Chris, the day that I come into my own, I'll be a monster."

I never took the Connecticut bar. We had three weeks to move to New Jersey and to find a house before Chris started selling chemicals. I had to find a new job, unpack, and make plans to practice law in New Jersey rather than Connecticut. Chris kept telling me that this year would be better and the sooner I became a member of the New Jersey bar, the sooner my self-confidence would return. I was fool enough to believe him.

We found a modest house, Chris started selling, and I began interviewing several law firms. One week later, I started at the firm of Goldman and Kessler for $40 a week.

The setup was entirely different from Legal Aid. Mr. Goldman was constantly in and out. My first task was to go through the one thousand files and see what had to be done on each case. Since I had no knowledge of the facts to properly analyze the cases, I resorted to arranging all of the correspondence and legal documents in chronological order. The job was routine enough to keep me busy during the first week.

I signed up in advance for the bar review course and received my materials. The pages were nine by eleven and stood in a pile a good seven inches high.

The next day when I walked into the office, Mr. Goldman eyed me curiously. "Is something wrong, Eda? You look like you've seen a ghost."

"I'll talk to you about it when you get back from court."

That night I waited for Mr. Goldman. I had to talk to someone about my fear of failure. It formed a welt in my stomach that made me choke at each promise of becoming a lawyer. I wanted to run, but instead I sat in the office at five o'clock peeling my dirty fingernails. In his usual kind way, Goldman turned his basset-hound eyes up and said: "Yeeeeesss? Trouble with that good-looking husband of yours?"

"No. I'm worried about taking the bar exam."

"You should be, my dear, and you should start studying right now."

"I have. But I don't think I'm going to pass it the first time around."

"So you don't pass. Christ. I flunked the first time and how do you think I felt? My wife was already a practicing member of the medical profession and I was a nothing. Try like hell to pass it the first time, kid. It's very demoralizing if you don't. I went a whole year telling myself that I was a no-good piece of shit and then I passed the second time. Now I make lots of money and I love it. Don't worry. If you don't pass, we aren't going to fire you."

"But I didn't tell you that I've been in the hospital for a nervous breakdown. I was seeing a psychiatrist up until the move to Jersey, and I'm thinking of taking off an hour of work to see if I can't find one in Paterson."

"See a headshrinker? Eda, you don't need to go see one of those nuts. You need to hit the books. Everyone goes through the same thing with the bar exam. I'll be your psychiatrist, kid. You can take off from work early if you want to study. I'll even help you go over some of the questions."

"I'd appreciate that, but I don't think you have the time."

"As I said, sweetheart, don't worry whether you're going to pass or not. Just get yourself in shape to take the exam. Maybe you're not cut out to be a trial lawyer. It's a tough business. Maybe you ought to consider a government job. This stuff can give you an ulcer if you take it too seriously."

After that interview, I decided to drop the whole idea of finding a psychiatrist, even though I felt the desperate need for outside help. Chris advised that I start reviewing right away. Every night when I came home from work, I'd mix cocktails and he'd read me the review questions while I tried to memorize the answers. I was supposed to be studying, but I wasn't going to skip my drinks in the evening. In Connecticut I usually had wine, but by now we had graduated to double Manhattans. I would skip my evening dosage of tranquilizers and sail off in a crooked line toward the bedsheets.

As the beginning of the bar review course drew nearer, I tried contacting a few doctors on my own and went to see one. I told him the whole story about Easton Park and went home to tell Chris that this new doctor wanted to see him. Chris breathed a deep sigh and took an extra gulp of his drink.

"Eda, I thought that just this once you could be on your own. Mr. Goldman has told you that he would help you with the bar exam questions."

Chris went with me to see the new doctor. We sat in the waiting room looking out of the window in the uncomfortable silence of incompatibility. He was called in first. Later, the doctor recommended that I come three times a week, and after continued therapy, I might be able to take the exam.

When we left the doctor's office, I expected the worst.

"I'm going out for a drink. You can come with me or I'll take you home."

"You're mad about the doctor, aren't you?"

"Three times a week! Hell, you don't even know this guy. Do you realize what he'll be taking you for?"

"Maybe he can help me."

"That's the goddamn trouble. You think that everyone can help you. Come, I'll take you home."

"No. I'm going with you. I don't care if you're angry."

"I'm not angry. I just want a drink. If it weren't for all those goddamn doctors interfering in my life, we might get along okay."

We drove into downtown Paterson and stopped in a lounge at one of the hotels. Chris ordered two Manhattans.

"I can't talk to you about doctors, Eda. This guy is very willing to take your money. So he'll listen to you three times a week and that's the only reason he'll see you. He's a smooth businessman, this one."

"Then I won't go. Drop the subject. It's finished. That makes me your sole responsibility. I didn't want to do things that way, Chris. I wanted the help of some doctor to get away and out from under all of you."

We ordered a second Manhattan. I hadn't eaten anything since morning, and the room began to spin. I was getting sick to my stomach but didn't tell Chris. Instead, I ordered a third drink and passed out before it was ever delivered.

The next thing I knew, I was lying in a bed of vomit and the alarm was buzzing. Now, by God, I wanted a doctor.

"Chris, I want to go to the hospital. I'm sick. Look at me, man. I'm dirty. I'm stinky and I'm low. Give up on me, Chris, I'm not worth it."

"Eda, it will be all over once you take the bar exam. Don't you have any guts?"

"Chris, I'm sick of life and half drunk. I need help."

I let him get ready for work and then went into the closet. I opened the bottle of tranquilizers and took about thirty. There was no other way out.

"Chris, I just took thirty tranquilizers."

"You what?"

"I go out and get drunk; I sleep in my own vomit. How much more vile can life get? I want to die, Chris. I'm twenty-six years old and I want to die. Go find Eva, Chris."

"Come over here to the sink." Chris got me to vomit half of the pills.

"Here we go again. Just tell me the name of the hospital and we'll get you admitted as a case of attempted suicide. It has to be reported, you know."

"Butler Memorial."

"Is it close? Goddamnit, we have to get your stomach pumped."

"Don't say that, I'm going to die."

"You're going to have your stomach pumped. Bring a nightgown."

We went immediately to the emergency entrance where the attendants put me on a table. I kept telling the attendant: "Chris's leaving me."

"No he's not. He's right here."

"No. Chris's leaving me because I'm no-good and I've been to the hospital too many times. I just wanted to see a doctor. That was all. I'm sick and I need help."

"Don't worry. You'll get it."

"Chris, will you come to see me?"

Chris turned his tired green eyes toward the floor. He'd given up with tears.

I sobbed to the nurse: "It's either him or the doctors. I can't have both."

"You'll be all right, dear. They'll take very good care of you at this hospital."

"But he doesn't love me anymore. I cause nothing but trouble."

After pumping my stomach, the nurse ushered me into the intensive care ward where I fell asleep. When I awoke, I asked one of the nurses for a cigarette.

"There's no smoking in this unit. You'll soon be transferred to another ward. Only the terminal cases stay."

Chris came that afternoon. Although his shoes were polished, his suit pressed, his hair combed, the deep lines under his eyes revealed the strain of long hours and little sleep.

"Chris, I won't take any more pills."

"You're right. I threw them away."

"I'll try to reform."

"You'd better if you want to take the bar exam."

"What are they going to do with me?"

"Transfer you to a mental ward for rest and rehabilitation, I suppose. Eda, if you'd only told me."

"You left me no alternative. I merely wanted help."

"Now you've got all the help in the world. I'll help you until the bar exam and then you're on your own."

"You mean you haven't given up with me?"

"You're in a low. Once you've passed the bar, you'll have some confidence in yourself."

That afternoon, I was ushered into another ward for mentally disturbed patients. I requested the doctor that we had visited in Paterson. In our first interview he asked me why I had taken an overdose. I explained the aftermath of the visit to his office and told him it would all be over once I took the bar exam.

The doctor was firm. "Mrs. Spaight, you're in no shape to take any exam. You'll stay here until you recover. At one time you call me up and say that it's an emergency. I arrange to see you and then you cancel the appointment because your husband is against therapy. Do you want to stay in the same rut that you're in right now? You have to follow my advice or I can't treat you as a patient."

"I'll stay. But you could keep me here forever. I have no medication and can't sleep at night. There's nothing to do but pace the halls, eat, and smoke."

"That's what you need—rest. You could stand to gain a few pounds too."

Those were the magic words. I picked at the food from there on in. I got on the scales every day just to be sure that I was losing weight. Butler Memorial was nothing like Easton Park. I paced the halls continuously, hung around the nurses' desk until I was asked to leave, and played Ping-Pong with every attendant I could find. There were no programmed talks among the patients. My doctor came only once a week, so I couldn't see how my "rest" was doing me any good. It was my third time on a mental ward, so I wasn't sure of doctors, patients, or anyone. I was convinced that Chris was hanging on until I took the bar exam. My parents called and conveyed their condolences that I was in the hospital again. Papa said to stay home and have a family like everyone else. Chris said nothing but was anxious about the bill.

"Eda, how long will you stay here?"

"As long as the doctor says, I suppose."

"What are they going to do? Give you pills to make you feel better?"

"I don't know. It's a different setup."

"You ought to know, Eda. You've been in enough hospitals."

"Maybe if I listen to this doctor, I'll feel well enough to take the bar exam."

"He may talk you out of taking it."

"Chris, the only way for me to take it is by having a doctor to talk to and relieve the strain."

"Confidence, Eda, confidence."

"Chris, bring me in my law notes. I'll study here."

So Chris brought in my notes. I read all the questions and answers over and over. But since I hadn't reasoned or figured anything out on my own while on amphetamines, I resorted to flipping the pages and attempting to memorize the answers. Every time Chris came, I was hounded by the same old question: "Eda, did you learn anything? Do you want me to help you with your notes?"

I stayed at Butler Memorial three whole weeks before I was finally discharged A.M.A. (Against Medical Advice). The doctor had only seen me twice, and every time he came, I asked to be let free. I had spent days in the kitchen begging to do the dishes and many sleepless nights pacing the halls. Most of the patients were elderly and didn't have the problems that I had. I had also lost weight.

In the meantime, the bills had been piling up. Seeing the doctor once a week did absolutely no good. Like Chris, I had begun to suspect that three times a week on the outside was money-motivated, since the doctor came only once a week when I was available.

On two afternoons when I asked to be discharged, the doctor came to see me. He was worried.

"Mrs. Spaight, you've only been here three weeks. What do you expect to have accomplished in that amount of time?"

"Nothing, I'm always waiting to see you."

"The purpose of therapy is to find out what you're like. I didn't want to send you to the hospital in the first place. What does your husband think about your leaving?"

"He thinks that the hospital is doing me no good at all. It's all a result of the bar exam."

"What do you think?"

"I want to go home. I can't get to see my husband who loves me."

"You have to give up some things for the sake of feeling better. Your husband's loving care isn't going to straighten you out."

"So I should give up my husband, and follow what you say with no guarantee that I get well. Then when I'm well, I've lost the one person who was worth getting well for. That won't work."

"If I gave you the medication, would you feel better?"

"Yes, but I really don't know what to do. Are you going to give me shock treatments? I'm afraid, because no one tells me what they're going to do with me. I'll stay if you give me something to calm me down."

Chris came that afternoon and I changed my mind again.

"Eda, did you tell the doctor that you want to go home?"

"He's going to give me some medication so that I can stay."

"That's what you wanted or that's what you want *now?* You'd better get out of this guy's hooks. I even brought your suitcases. Make up your own mind, woman. You're driving me nuts."

"I'm going home right now."

I told the nurse to leave a message that my husband and I were leaving. We packed as fast as was humanly possible. Nevertheless, we were met by the doctor in the hall.

"Mrs. Spaight, I thought you had decided to stay."

"I've changed my mind."

"I just came from a meeting with the staff doctors. We decided that if you want treatment, you have to make up your own mind. We can no longer act as go-between with you and your husband."

Chris nodded his head in agreement. The doctor carefully folded his arms, crossed one leg in front of the other, and blandly looked across the room. He wasn't going to give me an answer. Chris had already given me his decision. I nervously opened my purse out of habit, remembered that I had no pep pills on hand, and snapped the clasp shut, swearing under my breath.

"I'm going, Doctor. I have to live with my husband, and you only think about me once a week in the office."

The doctor bit his lips. "Not any more, Mrs. Spaight. I'll sign you out against medical advice."

"You're angry at me, aren't you?"

"No. I feel sorry and afraid for you, that's all."

I returned to work the day after my discharge and everyone at the office was happy to see me. Mr. Goldman looked at me with his tired eyes and smiled: "And how are you, my dear? You look a little thinner."

"I'm going to take the bar exam."

"That's good to hear. You can even study at the office if you want to."

My reform didn't last long. Despite all the promises I had made to Chris, I needed relief from the destructive anxiety of flunking the bar exam. At night, I'd lie in bed, thinking about the monotony of going through case folder #872 or trying to digest Question #105 of the bar review material. If I flunked the exam, I could face another year of the same fruitless routine. The next step was down to the kitchen and into the bourbon. A few tight swallows out of the bottle and I was sufficiently diverted from my worries to sleep another two hours. When I went back to bed, Chris could smell the liquor on my breath.

"Another snifter? Eda, please. I wish you'd cut out this drinking at night. If you're worried, wake me up and we'll talk about it."

"That's all right, Chris; I'm very sleepy right now. See you in the morning."

At one in the morning I was up for another swig. Chris was asleep when I tiptoed back to bed. But he knew. He knew that I had beer for lunch, followed by coffee, followed by Manhattans before dinner and half a quart of bourbon during the night.

Later on, I made an ass out of myself in front of the neighbors. Chris suggested that I take a night off and go to the ladies' club. I didn't know many of the women in the area and decided to attend. I arrived early and sat down where the women were drinking coffee. One of them had a cocktail. I saw it and dropped the hint to the hostess, who brought me a martini.

I was introduced to Flo Wingate, an older woman who practiced law in New York.

"I hear that you're another lady lawyer," she said.

"Not yet, Flo. I haven't passed the bar. I'm terribly worried about it."

"I know, dear. It's rough. Nothing like it used to be twenty years ago. Do you intend to practice in New Jersey?"

"If I pass. I'm working for a firm right now."

I took a last swallow of my cocktail. Only fifteen minutes had passed, but things were beginning to swim. I was given a refill. It was nine o'clock when I finished. The words of the chairman faded as I slumped over in my chair, dropping a shoe which clanked on the floor. Flo saw my plight and offered me a ride home. Chris met me at the door, apologized to Flo, and carried me up to bed. The next morning he left early. I woke up late, called in sick at the office, and hurriedly fished through the bedstand drawer for a cigarette. Instead, I pulled out a crumpled sheet of paper. It was in Chris's handwriting. I opened it up and read:

Eda, I know you're confused and upset about our goals. Everyone is telling you what to do, and you're wondering whether you're doing the right thing. When we get married, honey, you can do what you want, and I'll be behind you. Whatever you do is right. I've never met a girl with so much ambition and talent. I love you, Eda, so much that you'll never know. I miss your laughter and bright personality. When we get married, I want you with me always. . . .

I put the letter down as my tears fell one by one, smearing the ink. I wanted my pep pills. I wanted to be the Eda that Chris wanted—the Eda that Chris knew. I wanted, but I didn't know how.

I showed up for work until the final days before the bar review course began. I was afraid to go to the first class, but drowned my fears with five shots of bourbon the night before.

As I tripped over the comforter in a semistupor, Chris whispered, "Eda, give yourself a chance. Don't destroy."

"Chris, I never learned any law," I drawled, "I memorized it. On those pills, I couldn't even learn to spell my name. But you know what a terrific memory I have. It's frightening to have to learn to reason again when I don't know how to think straight."

"Just cut out the booze and you'll be helping yourself."

I passed out that night and gagged on breakfast the next day. "I can't eat. The cereal just sticks in my throat like peanut butter."

"Honey, you've got to eat. You've lost about six pounds in the last month. Try an apple."

"I'm not hungry."

"You can't eat because of all the bourbon that you drink at night."

"I'm worried about driving down to Newark."

"Have another cup of coffee and you'll make it."

With eight cups of coffee I made it through the first bar review lecture. I wanted to tell myself that things were clearer, but all that I remembered were the names of the legal principles that I had memorized to pass certain courses.

During lunch I talked to a few of the students and asked them when they had graduated from law school. I had to know, to compare them with myself. Most of them had gone to school in New Jersey and had just graduated, while I had to make up four years of lost time and overcome my drug-impaired reasoning power. While the course was given I was tempted to camp at the YWCA and avoid the commute. But I couldn't bear the thought of being away from Chris for weeks at a time. I tried to save time during lunch by eating my sandwich with one hand and recopying someone else's notes with the other. The lecturer went too fast and I couldn't keep track of the legal principles involved. I was up at his desk every day asking him about the problems or the legal principle he had talked about in the lecture the day before. Finally he put both of his elbows on the desk, leaned over his notebook, and smiled sadly. "My dear. I told you before that the only thing that's going to kill you on this exam is your anxiety. You went to an excellent law school. You're an intelligent person and the only thing that you lack is self-confidence. I know you have the ability to do well from the way you discuss the problems. You're luckier than most of the fellows here."

"But I've had a nervous breakdown and I can't think straight."

"You aren't the only one. You've just got to pick yourself up again, if you want to be a professional. I've watched you. You're an excellent student."

I went to the bar review every day that it was offered and spent some of the time after the lectures reviewing with Pete. He was very good about lending me his notes and reexplaining the legal principles involved. I was fine while I was at the YWCA and studying with someone else.

But on my own I was helpless. Faced with the prospect of cramming all three years of law school into one six-week review on my own after I came home, I openly gave in to Manhattans. I would have two on returning home from the course while I sat stretched out on the living room couch under the pretense of reviewing my notes. Chris would come over, pick up some of the printed pages, and start reading me the questions.

"Eda, are those Manhattans helping you study?"

"I've got to calm down enough to concentrate, Chris. The other students talk law day and night just like I used to do. I don't now. I just worry whether I'm going to pass or fail."

"So start studying."

"I can't, Chris. I can't. Law school was the one chance that I had to learn anything and I blew it. I fooled myself; I fooled my parents; I fooled everybody. And now, I face the final test."

"You have no confidence in yourself, Eda."

"It's more than that. At work people told me that I did a good job. I didn't believe them because they might not know what a bad job is. The bar review teacher tells me that I have a terrific background from an outstanding law school. I don't believe him because the last doctor I saw told me that I was nuts."

"You won't feel this way once you take the exam."

"You're determined that I've got to take the exam?"

"Eda, I just want you to take it. Just stop running. It won't hurt you to fail once in your life."

I resolved that night to continue the course no matter what it cost me. Chris tried to ignore my drinking, but I soon went up to three quarters of a quart of bourbon on my nightly rounds alone. I never felt like eating and lost twenty pounds in six weeks. Since I never bothered to wash, pimples broke out on my face and back. It didn't matter; I had to pass that exam for Chris's sake.

Six days of review wasn't enough, so I agreed with some of the boys to listen to tapes of the lectures on Sundays. I couldn't stand reviewing on my own. I was continually wound up and impatient to get down to the YWCA. Chris begged me to stay home and offered to help.

"Eda, you waste at least two hours commuting when you could study here. I'll read you the questions like we did at the beginning of the course. Christ, I never get to see you."

"I'm going because I don't want you to see me with a Manhattan this afternoon. Down there, I've got four other kids to keep my mind on law and off liquor. Every time I look at a question I want to pour enough juice in my system to dull that part of my brain that repeats: FLUNK!"

"Then go, Eda. Someday, I'll get to see your smile across the breakfast table."

The last Sunday before the end of the course, I was running scared. I didn't eat any breakfast, decided to skip lunch and wait until I got home. I never made it on my own; I was escorted. On the last lap of the trip, I stopped at a restaurant a mile from the house, went into the bar and ordered a martini on the rocks. I watched the bartender pour straight gin into a double container that sparkled under the reflection of the ceiling tensors, twisted my legs around the bar stool, and leaned my elbows on the polished mahogany shelf thinking: "Why not one stiffie, Eda, before you go home and face the old man?"

I started to talk to a salesman who was sitting next to me and I ordered another drink. Soon the ceiling tensors began to fade and the figures at the bar became blurred. Someone was carrying me and talking. A motor was running. The next thing I knew, I was in bed. Chris was wiping off my face, and I passed out. That night when I got up to go down for some bourbon, a hand caught my arm.

"Eda, after what you did tonight?"

"What?"

"Don't you remember? The owner of the restaurant carried you home, you vomited, and I just finished cleaning it up. You slammed against the wall downstairs and broke that little medallion that was given to us as a wedding present. Oh, no, my dear, you don't drink tonight. I can't take it any more, Eda. I'm a nervous wreck about my job as it is, I want out of this, woman. When was the last time you ever said anything happy?"

We had three days off before the exam. During that time, I kept repeating Chris's words to myself as I drank my precious bourbon in the morning: When was the last time I said anything happy? He had now lost all faith in me. Liquor had become a solo game. After he left in the morning, I'd pull out the bottle and get on the phone to Mom.

"I need your help, Ma. I'm drinking."

"Dear, get in touch with someone who can help you. Is there something I can do?"

"No, Chris would think it's interference. I want to go to a doctor, Ma. I need some kind of help—any kind. I called Alcoholics Anonymous today. I'm an alcoholic, Ma. But Chris thinks it will all be over once I pass the bar exam. It won't though."

Papa called that night. Orders were to let me see a doctor. Chris slammed down the receiver.

"Eda, I never said you couldn't see a doctor."

"No. But every time that I come home, there you are with a great big drink in your hand."

"Eda, half of your problems are made up."

"I'm an alcoholic."

"You're just looking for another excuse not to take the bar exam. You don't have to take it, Eda. I don't care."

"You must hate me."

"No, Eda. It's the other way around. I loved you so much that I took care of you in and out of three hospitals: the first for a nervous breakdown; the second for a nervous breakdown, and the third for an attempted suicide. For the past three years, I've been telling myself that you'd get better. Then I get calls from your parents telling me to take you to a doctor. I come home every night and find you plastered. I begin to think that I was mistaken and that you never really cared. I loved you, Eda, but now I have only pity. You call up all these people to help you and you never help yourself. Next week, when this bar exam is over, I'm through. You'll have to find your own niche in life."

Chris was right. I didn't care for him anymore because

I hated myself. I hated to get up and look in the mirror each day. I didn't want to live, but I kept telling myself that things would get better.

Then next day, Chris woke me up with a cup of coffee. "Well, today's the big day, kid. Do you think that you're up to it?"

"I want to die. I don't want to go to the exam."

"Say something happy for once. Aren't you going?"

I straightened up in bed, took a deep breath, and forced a smile. "Damn right, Chris. I'm going down to that exam and knock 'em dead. But I don't want to."

"Then do it for me, Eda. After that, you can go to all the doctors that you want."

When I arrived for the bar exam, the place was jammed with students. While I was waiting in line to register, I met a black student from Harvard who had already taken the exam once. We started talking about law schools and then went to lunch. I ordered a beer to calm my nerves.

"You're drinking beer on the day of the bar exam? That's cool. Where do you get your nerve?"

"I don't have anything but nerves."

I followed the beer with a cup of coffee, but both had dulled my brain. I walked into the exam, opened my blue book, and drew a complete blank. I tried to write, but the lecturer's words kept resounding like waves of hollow chains, clanking back and forth: "You've a lot of talent, my dear. You know the material. You went to a good law school and you've got the brains. The only thing that will ruin you is your own anxiety."

I looked at the first question and started outlining. Our lecturer had advised against it, but I had to do something besides look around at the other students. My nerves were catching up with me, and my hands began to sweat. I dropped my pen on the floor, got up and signed out for a smoke in the hallway. As I lit my cigarette, I glanced up and saw the sign for the bar downstairs. Slowly, like a wound-up mechanical toy, I propelled myself through the gate and down the steps toward the multicolored bottles that sparkled on the mirrored shelves in the lounge. I sat down in one of the plush velvet chairs and quietly ordered a Manhattan with a resolve not to tell Chris that I was killing myself. I would lie to him for the first time since I had been on pills. I would tell him all systems were go. I ordered another drink while I waited for a sandwich.

Chris would know that I tried my best. I ate the sandwich and went into the ladies' room to lie down. When I awoke, I had a cup of coffee, stalled around until exam time was up, and then drove home.

"Got a drink for a tired soldier?"

"Eda, you deserve it. How did the exam go?"

"Well, very well."

"Did you answer all of the questions?"

"To the best of my legal ability."

"See, I told you that you would hold up a lot better once the exam started."

"I'm not studying tonight, Chris. They always tell you to relax before the next day of the exam."

"I'm so proud of you, Eda. You made it."

I excused myself and went to the bathroom while Chris was mixing the drinks. I sat on the toilet, wiping my eyes and shaking my head. I coudn't look him in the face anymore since I had lied. I took a big snifter that night and went to bed dead drunk.

The next day I stayed in the exam room for the entire session. Since I didn't drink, I was miserable. I couldn't outline the problems. I began writing feverishly on any subject that I thought might pertain to the main issue. When the bell rang for lunch, my page was only half filled. I met the black friend from Harvard at lunch, and he noticed that I wasn't drinking beer.

"No, it didn't help," I murmured.

"Boy, you sure have a poor attitude about yourself."

"Yes, I need to see a doctor. I'm an alcoholic."

"Take it easy. If you flunk the first time, so what?"

I was determined to flunk the first time. I hadn't answered the questions from the first day and knew that I was dead. I downed all the bourbon in the house that night. The next day Chris left for work and I couldn't get the car started. Under the pretext that I had to go and get some groceries, I conned a neighbor into driving me down to the local A & P where I bought another fifth of bourbon. I wasn't going to the goddamn exam. I dialed Mom.

"Ma, I'm drinking, but it's the last day."

"Eda, at nine in the morning? No."

"That's okay. I'm calling my friends from Alcoholics Anonymous. I have to get out of this mess. Chris thinks it's all a sick joke."

"Why don't you come up to Syracuse and take a rest?"

I really didn't need a rest. I hadn't gone through the real anxiety of taking a test that I wanted to pass. I sideswiped the whole issue by getting drunk. I wanted my pep pills back. I wanted to be happy again. I slept in the afternoon and was too ashamed to tell Chris that I didn't go to the exam.

"I'm proud of you, Eda. You did it."

"Yeah, but I'm not going back to Goldman and Kessler."

"You don't want to be a lawyer?"

"I was nothing but a super file clerk. I'm going to look up that government job in Newark. I also want to see a doctor."

"You don't need one."

"Just look at me, man, and tell me what you see. My face and back are welts of pus. I weigh a hundred and ten pounds and drink bourbon like a fish. My clothes stink of sweat. I could really be a knockout if I care, but I don't have the ambition to give a shit. I need some peace."

"You mean that you want some medication?"

"I mean that I want to see Dr. Liebowitz."

"Where is he? You don't know how much he costs."

"I've located him in New York City. I'll pay for him."

"Another doctor."

"My parents have also invited me up to Syracuse for a rest. I think I'm going to take the time off and go."

"You're starting to run again, Eda."

"Leave the doctor to me. I won't ask for your approval anymore."

"What's he going to do for you? That's all I want to know."

"I haven't talked to him yet. Every time that I go, I worry about what you're going to be drinking when I get back."

"What are you going to do in the meantime?"

"Look for a job that pays."

That afternoon I called Liebowitz in New York and made an appointment. He remembered my case. Chris went with me. We entered the office and sat down.

"It's been a long time, Eda. What's the trouble?"

"Chris will tell you. My marriage is on the rocks, and I've flunked the bar exam."

"Doctor, she doesn't know that she's flunked the exam."

"I need help. I want to go to the hospital."

"But, Eda, the hospital isn't necessarily the answer."

"Chris didn't want me to come here in the first place."

"Eda, let's go back. The last time I saw you, you were about to be discharged."

"Things didn't work out. Chris is tired of my drinking and accomplishing nothing. I want to go to the hospital."

"Chris, would you agree to Eda's coming here for treatment—say on a once-a-week basis?"

"If that's what she needs, Doctor. I don't place much faith in the psychiatrists anymore, but I trust you as a person."

"Do you want out of your marriage, Chris?"

"I want out of my situation, Doctor. It's been very difficult to live with Eda the past three years. I've waited and hoped. We've gone from doctor to doctor, off pep pills, on pep pills. I'm also worried about myself. It has nothing to do with Eda. I'm dissatisfied with my job. I want to quit and go back to school. I don't think I'm cut out to be a salesman. I don't have the dedication. This is the second time that something like this has happened to me. I was in the navy for four years and wanted out. Although Eda's hospitalization was a tragedy, it gave me an excuse to get out of the navy. I started this selling job two years ago so that I could stay close to her. I don't like it. Instead of selling the plating chemicals, I get hung up at the shops solving their engineering problems. My customers like me, but I can't sell. I never discussed this with Eda."

"Do you have any ideas about school, Chris?"

"I've been toying with the idea of going back to graduate school for my Ph.D. in nuclear engineering. I got a good background while I was in the navy."

"The first time that I talked to you two, I thought you were both very idealistic."

"I'm going to look for a job, Doctor."

"I think that's a better idea than going into the hospital, Eda. Before our next meeting next week, think about what you can do for Chris."

I started looking for a job that week. I combed the want ads with no idea of what I wanted to do and no faith in my capacity to handle any of the jobs that were advertised. I went to see Liebs alone the next week.

"Eda, you called me three times last week. I refuse to stand between you and your husband."

"It's been this way since my discharge. Chris thinks there's nothing wrong with me. He forgets what I was like in the hospital."

"If you keep acting out like this, I'll have to put you in the hospital, although I don't want to. Hospitals don't solve anything. How is your job-hunting going?"

"Chris thinks that I'd be better off with a law job."

"I'm not convinced that you have the interest, Eda. You've only gone through the motions of taking the bar exam. What about all the languages that you speak? Why not get a nine-to-five job that's routine and leaves time for other, more creative things?"

"I have no interests, Doctor. I really want to give the whole thing up and go back to my parents."

"That's the root of your problems. Keep looking for a job, even though you don't feel like it."

"I have two interviews next week. They were begging for lawyers at one of the government agencies down in Trenton. I've also applied for the job of title searcher."

"Good. How's Chris doing?"

"Badly. He feels guilty about my father paying the doctor bills."

"How do you feel?"

"I'm glad Papa's got the money."

"I'll see you next week. In the meantime, take the medication I gave you and don't miss the job interviews."

That Monday, I went down to the title company. They offered $170 a week. On my third day of interviews I talked to Mr. Bullock from one of the government agencies in Trenton. They were willing to start me off at $9,600 a year. I told him nothing of my past. He was such a strong individual that I felt compelled to talk up to his standards. I said I'd let him know in a few days and went home to bring the good news to Chris.

"Why, Eda! That's the most that anyone has ever offered you! Are you sure that you don't have to be a member of the bar?"

"Sure as hell, man. You can quit your job and do whatever you want. They train me for the job. That's a lot different from Goldman and Kessler where I was left by myself all day. I think I'll take it."

"What time will you have to get up in order to commute down to Trenton?"

"Early, very early—maybe three A.M. if I want to leave a clean house. But I'll do it. This is the one chance I've got to make something out of myself. Mr. Bullock says he likes girls with guts."

"What are you going to put down on the application on the mental health question?"

"Normal."

"Is that what Liebs says?"

"Yes. Why ruin my chances from the start? Chris, I give you my word. I know it isn't worth much right now, but wait and see."

"Will you give up drinking?"

"No. But I won't be able to drink very much if I have to get up at three in the morning and go to work."

"What about Liebs?"

"I'll go on Saturdays."

That afternoon I had called Madge—one of the former patients at Easton Park. I wanted to talk to someone who might understand the agony of adjusting to life on the outside. Her mother answered the phone. Madge had been in the hospital again for attempted suicide and chronic alcoholism combined with habitual use of tranquilizers. She had been in and out of the hospital three times since my discharge and each time came out more depressed. Her husband got a divorce and left her with the custody of their five-year-old girl. I offered my sympathies after a brief chat about my job interviews and hung up. I saw enough similarity to my own pattern of behavior to know that the same thing was going to happen to me if I didn't shape up. This new job was my last chance.

The first day of work was disappointing. I needed something to keep me busy and spent the whole day chatting with my desk mate Guy Hamilton. He was good-looking, compatible, and expressed a great interest in passing the bar exam the next time that it was offered. It reminded me of the horror that I had just been through. I switched subjects and hounded him with questions about the job. I was still at the point of relying on others rather than making up my own mind about what to think. But I changed rapidly.

When I came home from work that night, I asked Chris for a cup of coffee.

"I had your Manhattan all ready."

"Can't drink, man. I'm bushed, but I have to get up at three tomorrow and go to work. I like the people."

"How can you tell, Eda? It's too soon."

"Not too soon. I'm only worried that I don't know the stuff."

I went to work the next day and every day for a year. I grew rapidly. I learned to think and reason. When I discovered that I could reason as well as most of my peers,

I didn't know what to do. The feeling gave me confidence but not satisfaction.

I also decided to take an interest in my appearance. I went to a cosmetic house in New York for a series of facials and followed the instructions about washing my face every night and applying cleansing lotions. I hadn't washed my face regularly in years. Slowly, I began to establish a regular routine—without a doctor's advice, and geared to my own strange needs.

In the meantime, Chris deteriorated. He would come home, listen to my reports of the job, fix a martini, and be out by the time I got dinner ready. On Sundays when he had to do reports for the company, he would start with Manhattans in the afternoon, take a long nap just to get away from it all, and then keep up the drinking until bedtime. I was still going to Liebs and I discussed this with him.

"Now that the roles are reversed, how do you like it, Eda? Your husband put up with this for three years. Why don't you tell him to quit the job and you'll support him if he decides to go to graduate school?"

"I don't know what else I can do. It's dragging me down to come home from work every night of the week and find him zonked out in bed and too drunk to even say hello."

"This time he needs your help."

"I told him that he ought to come and see you, but he refuses."

"Eda, a lot of people believe that doctors can't help them."

"I've told him, and I'm family. It's just like drugs and Papa. I'd lie only because he didn't trust me. The only thing that's keeping me off pep pills right now is the idea of writing a book about the hell I went through."

"Have you talked the idea over with Chris?"

"He's very enthusiastic about it."

"I'll talk to him next week if you think that it will do some good."

I returned home and told Chris that I was taking him with me the next week to see Liebs. He refused.

"Then quit, man. Quit the goddamn job and do whatever you want. Isn't that just what I did?"

"I don't know what to do, Eda. I think I'll call my parents tonight and talk to them."

I didn't say anything because I had done the same thing in the past. My own parents had tried. Mom had come out to Wisconsin with me to try and help me stay off drugs. When I had described this in my history of past hospitalization, Liebs pushed aside his notebook and eyed me curiously.

"Well! You never really recovered because you had a floating hospital. You had your mother to cook, clean, keep you company, and listen to your problems. You may have been a very independent person scholastically, but all the rewards were measured on your grades. Now it's your turn to be more realistic and help your husband."

"He has to decide what to do first. He doesn't listen to me."

"Did you ever listen to him when he told you to stop drinking before the bar exam? You're a tough cookie, Eda—a lot tougher than you think. Come back next week and tell me that you've started your book."

When we went to the doctor's office that next week, Chris assured him that I was the least of his worries. Liebs then turned to me and asked if I was willing to tighten up the purse strings for a year to put Chris through school. The idea gave me a feeling of independence. But where was all the money going to come from? Liebs was sympathetic but firm. Papa was paying the doctor bills so there was nothing to worry about as far as treatment went.

I kept pushing Chris to quit his job. The company wasn't paying him enough. He wasn't like the other salesmen who threw out home and family when business called. One night I sat down and drew an example from my own past.

"Chris, remember when I wanted to be a practicing lawyer? I had great visions of going into court and fighting to the death. Then I got out on the job and I didn't go into the appellate courts. Right now I'm still doing routine things. It just isn't that easy to get to the top.

Dr. Liebs told me last Saturday that he even dinked around for two years before entering med school. Now look at what a good doctor he is. Maybe the whole bit about me being a lawyer was a product of pep pills. The idea was to be an 'Eda'—to be different from anyone else. I'm a lawyer but look at the high price that I paid: six lost years, two trips to the hospital on a long-term basis, one attempted suicide. Man, sit down and think before you do something that you hate."

"I'll have a talk with my boss tomorrow."

"He's going to tell you that you're a good man, that you ought to stick it out and that it's really too soon to tell. But you know right now that every day that you have to go to that job you feel sick inside. I used to feel that way when I went to the law office. I was ready to puke."

"Eda, it's not that easy to quit."

"It's very easy. Use me as an excuse. That company has had their eye on me from the very start because I won't support you in something that you don't like. I can't attend all the company functions and be 'rah-rah' because I have my own job. Besides, if you can't stand on your own feet without my constant help, then I don't want to stay married to you. I didn't marry a baby like Papa."

Chris quit his job that week and decided to go back to school in nuclear engineering. He applied to several universities in the area and finally chose Columbia. He also won a scholarship, so we had no worries about money.

In the meantime, I was still going to Liebs. As I became stronger, conflicts between Chris and me arose. I went from buying nothing to filling three closets. I wore makeup that I ordered in New York and that was expensive. I never gave a crap about the opinions of others while I was on pep pills. Now I began to wonder if things weren't going too well for me. Even though I got up at three every day, I processed more cases than most of the people who sat around me. I gained a reputation as an expert in the work that I was doing. I did all the Spanish and Italian translations for the office in addition to my regular case load.

I told all this to Liebs at our next meeting.

"Doctor, when am I going to fall?"

"Don't worry, Eda, as long as you know your own feelings."

"It's great to go to work in a new dress. I work twice as hard. Chris says that I buy too many. But I only buy bargains. Everybody looks at me and they don't look with disapproval. I like the feeling."

"You're a woman."

"But I like to flirt. I eat lunch with the boys. My boss winks at me and I wink back."

"You've got sex appeal. What's wrong with that?"

"I'm being disloyal to Chris."

"As long as you mean nothing by your flirting, don't worry. If others misinterpret what you say, that's their hang-up."

"But I also am attracted to other men who are good-looking or whose personality I like. My pulse goes like a bullet, needles of blood tickle my skin, and I always say the wrong thing, except to Hamilton, the guy I started my training with."

"You were never aware of these feelings?"

"I never had any feelings while I was on pills, and now I'm frightened. It makes me angry because a lot of people at the office talk—jokingly, of course. I'm frivolous and shallow. Why do I need the praise of my boss in order to feel good?"

"You need people. Just tell me when they tear you down for bad work. If it makes you feel good when men turn their heads or whistle, that's nothing to be afraid of."

"But I also want to be taken seriously. When it's business, I want to be accepted on the same level as a man. I have more brains than most people at work."

That week at work the assistant chief in the office asked me if I wanted to do a television show in Spanish on a New York channel. My division chief, Mr. Bullock, would accompany me down to the studio. He gave me the day off to get my hair done and told me to come in looking sexy, sleek, and smart.

That night I was ecstatic. I couldn't wait to bring the word home.

"Chris, sit down. Have a drink. We're going to celebrate."

"Celebrate what?"

"I'm going on TV next week for a whole half hour."

"Kiddo, looks like things are really picking up for you on the job."

"It makes a difference when you look sharp. They ask you to do things and represent the government, although I don't look like the typical government worker. I've got to call up Liebs and give him the good news."

My visits to Liebs were sporadic now. I scheduled an appointment whenever I felt that I needed him. In June, I walked into the office and sat down.

"I won't need you for the rest of the summer. I'm doing pretty well, although I'm somewhat discouraged. A whole new bunch of people have been hired. The only person that I can talk to is Hamilton. The older trainees have been moved to another unit. If it weren't for him, I'd go insane."

"You talk about Guy Hamilton a lot. You're attracted to him?"

"Yes, physically and emotionally. But I'm not going to do anything about it except feel guilty. I'm married and I'm not supposed to have feelings like that."

"Hogwash. Everybody has those feelings. It's what they do about them that makes a difference. Does Chris know?"

"Of course. I tell Chris everything. I was never interested in anyone this way when I was on drugs. Half of my feeling toward Hamilton is because I respect the quality of his work. He's the only one in my unit who's my equal. We're the only two that are asked to do overtime, even though Bullock knows that I don't need the money as much as the men with families."

"You feel funny about Hamilton because you're around six years behind in feeling your own femininity. All the time that you were on drugs you had no emotions."

"It'd all be okay if there were only the two of us. We respect each other and that's the only basis that I have for flirting. It's a game that I like to play. Hamilton likes to play it too. He purposely faces me in a crowded elevator at lip level and smiles or mumbles a great big 'uh-huh!' And he can't keep his eyes off the cleavage when I wear a low neckline. It doesn't take much to guess what he's thinking. The game is not saying what you think. But no one else in the office understands. They talk when we go out in the park to eat lunch. They talk when we take our coffee break together."

"Eda, everyone gossips. Besides, now you're being judged by other people's standards—not your own."

"Lower standards. It's no fun to be good-looking. Everybody thinks I'm a sexpot because I wear mini skirts and low-cut dresses—everybody that doesn't matter."

"You have a real hang-up about being accepted on a man's level."

"Well, why can't I be a knockout and still get respect for the quality of work that I do? My supervisor sees it that way. And so does Hamilton, but he's going to another division soon."

Liebs and I agreed not to meet during the summer. In September, I called him to schedule an appointment.

"Haven't seen you all summer. How are you?"

"Fine and tired. I haven't had a vacation in over a year and now that I'm getting one, it isn't exactly what I wanted."

"You're going to visit relatives and you'd rather be by yourself?"

"Exactly. We always go to see the relatives. I want to go someplace like Las Vegas. Chris says we don't have the money. Hell, I've got a fat savings account and stocks. I'm *rich*, and no one's going to get it after me."

"Don't you want children?"

"Not in the least. I couldn't stand to give up my career or my independence to be tied down to a house. I like kids but only at certain times. I'm too immature myself. Besides, Chris is going on for his Ph.D., and we need all the income we can get. He's more important."

"How does Chris feel?"

"He agrees. If I don't want a family, so what? When

your kids are grown up there's only two of you left anyway. Chris doesn't have any big thing about passing on the family name. He needs a partner, not a corporation."

"Someday you may change."

"I doubt it. You know how I feel about putting on a few pounds. When you're pregnant, you gain weight, get all out of shape. With my phobia about eating, I'd be tempted to go back on the pep pills in a hurry."

"Okay. Anyway, you could both use a vacation. How are things at work?"

"Rough. The case load is heavy, and I'm dying to get out of training and on to something that taxes my brain. I also had a small blow-up with the fellow who sits next to me. I've been authorizing this young lawyer for about two weeks. It takes time to review someone else's work, and his work isn't so hot. One day when he was out, I read over his mail in order to release it. Most of the letters were incorrect, so I took the trouble to redictate them on my own time which meant that my own production suffered. The next day, I offered him a copy of the redictated, corrected letters. He looked them over, threw them in the wastebasket, and said: 'Well, I'd rather do these things off the top of my head. After all, when I get into practicing law, I'll have to think on my feet!' I tried to explain that all of the letters were standard letters to be used in the particular cases at hand. Most of them had come out of congressional interest in these types of cases. My young friend couldn't be bothered. He turned to me and shouted, 'You're only a nine-to-five government worker. Why should you care? This is nothing more than a clerk's job. Why you're not even a practicing attorney or a professional.' By this time I was livid. 'Someday you'll learn, my silver spoon-fed baby,' I creamed, 'that even if you're a table busser or a garbage collector, you'd better be goddamn good at it. People pay for work, not brats with a label.'

"That was it. The kid was up from his chair and into the supervisor's office. He wanted to be moved. I was pretty angry myself. I've been putting up with this kid for too long. He had a few drinks at lunch one day and chewed up the marigolds on my desk. He has no interest in the job and yet has a chip on his shoulder because he's a lawyer.

"When the supervisor called me in, I was upset. I knew that this kid resented me because I have a reputation for knowing my work and being the best one in the unit. I was tired of hearing all these brats call my supervisor a jerk and the job a stupid waste of time. My supervisor said he wouldn't move me, so I walked around and came back to my seat.

"Chris said that I should have kept my mouth shut. Maybe, but it's murder to go to work and not talk to anyone all day long."

"Well, Eda, our time is almost up. Let me sum up. You shouldn't spend all your time visiting the relatives. You're still finding yourself and you need time away from other strong influences such as parents in order to get established. I don't think Chris realizes how much you've changed. If you blow up at work and can come out smelling like a rose, so much the better. Don't be quiet if something is bothering you. Evidently, they're pleased with you and want you to say what you think. As for getting pregnant, it's your business and I wouldn't listen to other people on the blessings of raising a family. Why don't you go to Las Vegas?"

"I'm going. Chris got straight A's this semester and he needs a break too. By the way, I need another prescription of Stelazine. I'll give you another call when I've finished the book and am up for promotion."

I scheduled an appointment with Liebs on my return home from Las Vegas. I drove into the city, had a cup of coffee and plopped down in my favorite chair at his office. Work was on my mind and so was Chris.

"Well, Doctor, I'm alone. Hamilton left for another division. The boys don't ask me to go with them for coffee anymore. They all go together. I think they resent me."

"Because you've been there the longest and know more?"

"Of course I could pretend that I don't know that much."

"No, Eda. You've moved up and been given a favored position because of the quality of your work and your personality. You're well liked."

"Yes, but when I'm favored by my supervisor, I make enemies. The boys all group together."

"That's what's called the 'herd instinct.' You either stay with those who are your contemporaries or you stand out and go it alone. You will be resented for a while, but give them a chance to accept your position. What about Guy Hamilton?"

"The whole thing's over with. I got burned. I don't get burned very often but I learned."

"What happened?"

"I had a dinner party before I went to Las Vegas. I wanted Guy to meet my husband because I thought Chris might enjoy him. I invited Guy, his wife, and another couple over for dinner. I went all-out. My best china, hand-cut crystal, my sterling—the works. Guy's wife seemed to have a good time talking to Tina and myself when I wasn't arranging things. After that I never heard 'Boo.' I never got an acknowledgment, or a thank-you note. I felt damn funny about it. I talked to Tina about it later. The same thing happened when Guy passed the bar. Two other girls at work and I agreed to chip in and buy Guy a bottle of champagne. None of us ever got a thank-you note or anything. After that, I crossed him off my list. Tina says that maybe there was a little jealousy or mistrust on the part of his wife. I don't know, but I feel bad. When she had been over, I purposely didn't talk about work. I talked about my baking, cooking, sewing, embroidery, and all the other things that I do. Some of the boys often go to see Guy in the other division."

"And you?"

"I have no reason. Anything that I see him on will be business. I think I attributed more to him than he was worth. I often do that and then I become disappointed in people. That's why I spend so much time by myself."

"Do you eat lunch by yourself?"

"No. I eat with two girls that I met in training. I don't think that I gave one of them a chance. I was too busy with Guy. She understood but said nothing—mark of a mature person. Since Hamilton left, I've enjoyed talking to her about all we have in common. We like nice clothes. She likes to travel, and I can talk ideas too. I don't have very many people that understand me, but I think she does. She accepts me anyway. I prefer being with men, but that's one girl I don't mind being with."

"How was Las Vegas?"

"I loved it, but Chris worried about money the whole time. By the way, I think I've found a cleaning lady. Chris's worried about that too. He doesn't think we can afford her. Hundreds of thousands in the bank and I can't afford eleven dollars a week for a cleaning lady. I never did hear the end of Las Vegas and the money we blew out there. Chris is very much like Papa. Papa now has millions of dollars and he's still trying to figure out how to make more in the stock market. He couldn't spend all that money in his lifetime if he tried. But he keeps telling Chris and me to hang on to the stock, never sell the principal and never invade corpus."

"That sounds senseless."

"I agree. If I have money, I like to spend it. I work hard for the money I make. Every time that Chris and I get in a hassle, it's over all the new clothes that I buy or the money that I spend on spices for my gourmet cooking or on gardening. He wants me to save it."

"That's just about impossible since he isn't working."

"I know. I've got it good now and I'm enjoying it. I use all the oddball cooking equipment that I buy. I plant all the plants that I pick. I read all the books that I order. I've been through hell on this earth for the past six years and now I'm starting to find heaven. I want heaven. I want all the things that keep me going, keep me happy, and keep me alive. Life is more fun than when I was on drugs. It's a lot harder, but I want it that way."

As winter came on, and my job increased in difficulty,

I soon realized how much I had changed. I started baking again. I thought that by making my food more interesting, I might like the taste and overcome the whole phobia I had about eating. I would get up early on Saturdays to bake yeast bread. On Sundays, I would bake four different kinds of cookies. Since my sister had a baking business in Rochester, I would try different kinds of cookie recipes and send them off to her. Then I would leaf through one of my fifty cookbooks to find some main dishes that I could make ahead and freeze. I'd bake about six main dishes for use during the week since I was getting home late and wanted to spend time on the book. Baking was a release from the increased tensions that I felt at work. Besides, I liked to experiment. I was finding out that I was basically a dabbler. When I baked, I baked up a storm. I went from basic breads to coffee cake and then to brioches, strudels, and sourdough specialties.

I asked my parents for a sewing machine that Christmas. I hadn't sewn in six years. I bought some material and made draperies for Chris's study. I had also started a tapestry out of crewel embroidery for Chris to hang on the wall. Since I had done a lot of crewel embroidery, I chose an advanced pattern with many new and difficult stitches. And for Christmas, I made a detailed angel out of wood and sequins for the front door. That was on the weekends. During the week, my spare time was devoted to finishing the book.

Chris was getting worried. "Eda, why don't you stop? Why don't you slow down and relax?"

"Why? I relax by doing. I get up early on Saturday mornings to bake bread because it's a blast. Watching the bread rise is creative. It's interesting. I've never done it before. That recipe that Aunt Gabriella gave me for Sicilian pizza is fun to follow. Now everyone in the neighborhood wants my recipe for Sicilian pizza."

"But, Eda, you bake enough for an army."

"So what? When I'm baked ahead, I have time to do other things—like finish the book."

"But you don't eat any of the bread that you make and

you don't touch the cookies. How do you know that they're good?"

"Because good stuff goes into them and other people say that the stuff I make is out of this world."

"Why don't you go visiting?"

"Who am I going to visit? I don't have many friends who have very much in common with me. I can only talk to my friend at work about cooking because she cooks the same way I do. If I've got something that calls for green ginger root or fenugreek seed, I won't be happy until I find them. I have so little time to relax and do gourmet cooking. All week long, I do what other people tell me to do. Now I'll do what I want to do. I'm thinking of selling the stuff that I make instead of giving it away. But that's in the future. By the way, I have to go down to Paterson and find some chorizos and longanizas. I'm cooking Mexican and Spanish this week. I'll need your help on that designer coat that I'm making. It's an uneven design like an unmatched plaid."

"I'll help you, but slow down."

"Chris, you've told me for the past three years that you'd like to see me off drugs. Are you getting the picture of what I'm really like? I'm afraid, too. I'm afraid to be so interested in everything. I'm an Eda that you've never known. The more I do of one thing that pleases me, the more I want to do. There's never enough time. I'm good at work. I have more ambition and intelligence than most of the men who have been on the job for twenty or thirty years. But I'm not going to be recognized for a while and that's frustrating. So, in the meantime, I can devote myself to all my other interests. I live when I write. I live when I bake brioche. I live when I get up on Sundays and make cookies and then go out for my two-hour bike ride, all by myself, alone with my God—damn Him when it snows."

"Eda, you don't have to swear."

"Why shouldn't I? My Lord understands. He's completely wigged out, man. I swear at Him occasionally, talk, pray, mumble, and complain. He makes sure that my bread rises, my plants grow, and not too many tulips are eaten up by the moles."

"Eda, you're talking nonsense."

"Am I? No. I'm Eda. I'm different. Before I die, I will live as I have never lived before. I will work until I scream from exhaustion. I'll bake until my arms ache from kneading the dough; I'll sew until my fingers are stiff from so much stitching. I'll write until my mind lapses from fatigue. But I won't quit this mad, crazy world again."

I went to Dr. Liebowitz's office that next week for a short visit.

"I'm worried, Doctor."

"Why?"

"Because a lot of changes have taken place since I saw you last. I'm up for the next promotion. I've found so many interests that Chris is worried about me. I wrote Mom a long letter last week saying that she was the only one who could understand what I was like six years ago. Now that I've gained six pounds and don't look like a skeleton, Chris and I are on good terms. He wouldn't talk to me when I weighed a hundred and ten pounds. He just kept looking at me. Now I don't trust him or anyone who tells me what I ought to weigh. I have more interesting things to do than worry about my weight.

"There's more. In my husband's eyes, I never relax. I get up to bake, sew, or bike ride on the weekends. I don't feel like wasting time. I have one friend at work who I enjoy and one neighbor who I like to talk to sometimes. I have nothing in common with most women my age and don't intend to change. They don't work and are concerned about their children. I'm interesting to them but they're not interesting to me. I can't get turned on about dirty diapers. My sister Stella is a different story. She has five kids and a baking business. She's another nut like me. I do things now because I like to, and Chris doesn't understand this. I'm very sensitive to his constant criticism and at times I burst into tears. I have a terrible inferiority complex. When I get going too fast, nothing is right. Our kitchen is too small for all the things that I make. Nothing is ever in the right place. I swear when I'm baking, but I'm still having a good time. I've become a monster."

"How is your father?"

"He just got fitted for a brace. He's got Parkinson's, you know."

"Why did I ask you that question?"

"I haven't the slightest. It doesn't seem to connect."

"It connects in this sense. All your life you've wanted to be recognized by your father for having done something of merit in his eyes. Now that he's too old or too sick, it must be frustrating to know that this will never come true. So you take it out on your husband when he offers the criticism. You're also tired of the routine and being the breadwinner. Now that you have confidence at work, you seek recognition from those who are higher in command."

"I love Papa but I will never be anything more to him than an unruly ten-year-old little girl who sat on his lap and asked him when he was going to marry me. I guess I realized that a long time ago. Papa's proud of me, but he'll never understand me."

"And Chris?"

"Maybe I've outgrown him."

"Have you ever said that out loud?"

"No. Because I'm not sure and I was afraid I might start to cry. Now look at me. I'm crying."

"Eda, let me explain and perhaps you'll feel more comfortable. For six years you did absolutely nothing. If charted on a graph, it would be a straight line. After you started this job and decided to change, the line started to go up. Now it's shot up in a straight perpendicular and is still rising. You haven't yet discovered your own limits. Chris, in the meantime, is at the straight-line level. He's still in school. Even though he got straight A's in nuclear engineering and faces qualifying exams for his Ph.D. this fall, you're in two different worlds. He may start to grow later on. I think you need more of his support."

"Doctor, I'm lonely. Do you know what it's like to reign in hell—to realize that you're faster and better than most people but somehow you just don't fit? To stand up and pay for it? I'm no angel and I don't make distinctions on the basis of education. A lot of the people at work that I like are in the lower positions. They're more fun because they aren't so impressed with giving an impression. Look, I'm going to go now. I need another prescription so that I can sleep at night. In the meantime, try the cookies I baked—macadamia nuts, pineapple and coconut. They're Hawaiian, a taste of Hawaii in every bite. I make them in my grass skirt."

"Go, Eda. You know yourself. That's more than a lot of people."

Epilogue

Knowing myself was one thing, but going back to life and my situation with Chris called for the courage of trying. In my case, I had no guidelines and no comparisons. Chris had only known me on drugs, and so I lived with the resentment of knowing that he didn't understand what I was really like. But I had to keep trying. Soon Chris received his masters in nuclear engineering and then he started a job in New York. Our life together was a series of constant adjustments, and his growth curve soon matched, crossed, and followed the rise of mine to new highs at the professional level. Responding to my need for intense physical activity and relaxation, Chris soon joined me on my bicycle rides, and his interest in summer and winter sports soon equaled my own. But life was still too easy, and I still had not found the challenge that I wanted.

Disgruntled and stifled by my job in government, I announced to Chris one evening that I was going to attempt the bar exam a second time. This time, I wanted a license to practice law, the key that would open up a new world, one that might satisfy my craving for fulfillment. I had been away from the study of law for six years, but I became devoted to the new undertaking. One year before Papa Franchi died, he cried to know that his daughter Eda had been admitted to the bar. I didn't do it for him, and I didn't do it for Chris. I did it for myself and that's why it worked.

I soon left government and entered the private practice of law. It was all and more than the challenge I had hoped it would be. Chris was promoted to a level of responsibility that devours the work week as well as the weekends. When we get together now, it is like an entire honeymoon in an hour. Because of both failure and success, we have each developed a sense of humor and a new, relaxed sense of harmony.

Both Chris and Papa had to realize that drugs are a personal problem. Drug addicts aren't violent people. They are sick people. But they still have half a mind left and that deserves recognition. Many may not want to be helped. Many may wish to stay high for the rest of their lives. Being high is a great feeling. It eliminates the problem of dealing with emotions, phobias, family tensions. But, in the long run, the price is just too great. I lost six years of my life.

My family background had a lot to do with drugs. My motive wasn't to take drugs for the fun of it, but to achieve. Any student who has a report to do or an exam to study for will probably pop a few dexies to stay up all night and study. He may flunk the exam or fall asleep the next day, but the pills will give him the drive and the confidence to go in to the exam, do a bad job, and let him think that he's going to come out with flying colors. In the same way, an average housewife who has taken a few diet pills may be the busiest person in the world. She will have the untapped energy to accomplish the tasks at hand and feel good when the physical work is done. Or a busy executive may take pills to keep going during the day; he may cool off with tranquilizers at night. All of these people are missing life. If they don't have the energy or the willpower to do something, they will miss more.

Although I have conquered my own addiction and passed the bar, I am still left with many conflicts. I am not a perfect person. I don't fully understand the hang-ups and the mistakes of the generation that reared me. Young people are fighting against the life-style of their parents. They don't want to accept the mundane world of nine-to-five jobs, bill paying, and routine. Drugs make it easier to put up with anything. So I don't condemn addicts. But I know better.

SIGNET Books of Interest

☐ **DRUGS, PARENTS, AND CHILDREN: The Three-Way Connection** by Mitchell S. Rosenthal, M.D. and Ira Mothner. The book you should read before it's too late! How to keep your kids off drugs, and what to do if they're already hooked. (#Y5391—$1.25)

☐ **MARIHUANA: A Signal of Misunderstanding; The Official Report of the National Commission on Marihuana and Drug Abuse.** With a special foreword by Raymond P. Shafer, Chairman. The most comprehensive study of marihuana ever made in the United States. Who smokes it? And why? Does it trigger crime? Harmful or innocuous? A psychic euphoriant? A sexual stimulant? The future of its medical and legal status?
(#Y5218—$1.25)

☐ **DRUG ABUSE AND ADDICTION: A Fact Book for Parents, Teen-agers, and Young Adults** by Barbara Milbauer. With an introduction by Richard Ottinger. A timely handbook for today's growing world of drug abuse and a closely researched report on every phase of drug-taking. (#Q4885—95¢)

☐ **THE HEROIN TRAIL** by the Staff and Editors of Newsday. This shocking, Pulitzer Prize-winning journalistic investigation tells the full story of the heroin traffic that begins in Turkey and ends in the graves of young American addicts—and names the men who grow rich on this merciless drug and turn blind eyes to its cruel and deadly punishments. (#J6281—$1.95)

THE NEW AMERICAN LIBRARY, INC.,
P.O. Box 999, Bergenfield, New Jersey 07621

Please send me the SIGNET BOOKS I have checked above. I am enclosing $_____(check or money order—no currency or C.O.D.'s). Please include the list price plus 25¢ a copy to cover handling and mailing costs. (Prices and numbers are subject to change without notice.)

Name_____

Address_____

City_____State_____Zip Code_____
Allow at least 3 weeks for delivery

Other SIGNET Titles You Will Enjoy

☐ **LISA, BRIGHT AND DARK by John Neufeld.** Lisa is slowly going mad but her symptoms—even an attempted suicide—fail to alert her parents or teachers to her illness. She finds compassion only from three girlfriends who band together to provide what they call "group therapy." (#Q6275—95¢)

☐ **LIE DOWN IN DARKNESS by William Styron.** An outstanding novel about a tortured girl and the people and events that lead her to the brink of despair.
(#Y5484—$1.25)

☐ **MR. AND MRS. BO JO JONES by Ann Head.** A deeply moving story of two courageous teenagers caught in a marriage of necessity. (#Y6446—$1.25)

☐ **FOR ALL THE WRONG REASONS by John Neufeld.** From the bestselling author of **Lisa, Bright and Dark** comes a tender, taut novel about a teen-age marriage that speaks to today. (#Y5786—$1.25)

☐ **KNOCK ON ANY DOOR by Willard Motley.** A bestselling novel, the moving portrayal of a sensitive boy who dreamed of the stars, but ended his brief lifetime of frustration and despair in the electric chair.
(#W5223—$1.50)

THE NEW AMERICAN LIBRARY, INC.,
P.O. Box 999, Bergenfield, New Jersey 07621

Please send me the SIGNET BOOKS I have checked above. I am enclosing $_____(check or money order—no currency or C.O.D.'s). Please include the list price plus 25¢ a copy to cover handling and mailing costs. (Prices and numbers are subject to change without notice.)

Name_____

Address_____

City_____State_____Zip Code_____
Allow at least 3 weeks for delivery

Have You Read these Bestsellers from SIGNET?

☐ **FEAR OF FLYING by Erica Jong.** A dazzling uninhibited novel that exposes a woman's most intimate sexual feelings. . . . "A sexual frankness that belongs to and hilariously extends the tradition of **Catcher in the Rye** and **Portnoy's Complaint** . . . it has class and sass, brightness and bite."—John Updike, New Yorker (#J6139—$1.95)

☐ **PENTIMENTO by Lillian Hellman.** Hollywood in the days of Sam Goldwyn . . . New York in the glittering times of Dorothy Parker and Tallulah Bankhead . . . a 30-year love affair with Dashiel Hammett, and a distinguished career as a playwright. "Exquisite . . . brilliantly finished . . . it will be a long time before we have another book of personal remembrance as engaging as this one."—**New York Times Book Review** (#J6091—$1.95)

☐ **THE FRENCH LIEUTENANT'S WOMAN by John Fowles.** By the author of **The Collector** and **The Magus**, a haunting love story of the Victorian era. Over one year on the N.Y. Times Bestseller List and an international bestseller. "Filled with enchanting mysteries, charged with erotic possibilities . . ." —**Christopher Lehmann-Haupt, N.Y. Times**
(#E6484—$1.75)

☐ **HARRIET SAID by Beryl Bainbridge.** An explosive shocker about little girls . . . here is the horror of child's play mixed with erotic manipulation and evil possession. "A highly plotted horror tale that ranks with the celebrated thrillers of corrupt childhood."—**New York Times Book Review**
(#W6058—$1.50)

☐ **DANCING MAN by Edward Hannibal.** From the author of the one-million-copy bestseller, **Chocolate Days, Popsicle® Weeks**—a novel that touches the most intimate emotions—a love story, moving and unforgettable. (#W6205—$1.50)

THE NEW AMERICAN LIBRARY, INC.,
P.O. Box 999, Bergenfield, New Jersey 07621

Please send me the SIGNET BOOKS I have checked above. I am enclosing
$_____(check or money order—no currency or C.O.D.'s). Please include the list price plus 25¢ a copy to cover handling and mailing costs.
(Prices and numbers are subject to change without notice.)

Name_____

Address_____

City_____State_____Zip Code_____

Allow at least 3 weeks for delivery

More Bestsellers from SIGNET

☐ **A CIRCLE OF CHILDREN by Mary MacCracken.** A moving story of how a teacher's dedication and love worked miracles with her emotionally disturbed children. "We finish the book shaken yet uplifted, for we have watched how love and understanding, working together, can produce what were once called miracles."—Clifton Fadiman, in **Book-of-the-Month Club News** (#W6354—$1.50)

☐ **HOUR OF GOLD, HOUR OF LEAD by Anne Morrow Lindbergh.** The Lindberghs were the golden couple in a fairy-tale romance. And when their first child was born, the world rejoiced. Eighteen months later, tragedy struck. . . . "A totally expressive, often unbearable record of an extreme personal anguish that followed the greatest possible happiness. Mrs. Lindbergh has a great gift for communicating directly her joy and pain."—**The New York Times Book Review** (#E5825—$1.75)

☐ **JENNIE, VOLUME I: The Life of Lady Randolph Churchill by Ralph G. Martin.** In JENNIE, Ralph G. Martin creates a vivid picture of an exciting woman, Lady Randolph Churchill, who was the mother of perhaps the greatest statesman of this century, Winston Churchill, and in her own right, one of the most colorful and fascinating women of the Victorian era. (#E5229—$1.75)

☐ **JENNIE, VOLUME II: The Life of Lady Randolph Churchill, the Dramatic Years 1895-1921 by Ralph G. Martin.** The climactic years of scandalous passion and immortal greatness of the American beauty who raised a son to shape history, Winston Churchill. "An extraordinary lady . . . If you couldn't put down JENNIE ONE, you'll find JENNIE TWO just as compulsive reading!"—**Washington Post** (#E5196—$1.75)

THE NEW AMERICAN LIBRARY, INC.,
P.O. Box 999, Bergenfield, New Jersey 07621

Please send me the SIGNET BOOKS I have checked above. I am enclosing
$_____(check or money order—no currency or C.O.D.'s). Please include the list price plus 25¢ a copy to cover handling and mailing costs. (Prices and numbers are subject to change without notice.)

Name_____

Address_____

City_____State_____Zip Code_____

Allow at least 3 weeks for delivery